DATE DUE

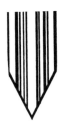

Immigration

IMMIGRATION

*Newcomers and Their
Impact on the United States*

Tricia Andryszewski

Issue and Debate
The Millbrook Press
Brookfield, Connecticut

Library of Congress Cataloging-in-Publication Data
Andryszewski, Tricia, 1956-
Immigration : newcomers and their impact on the United States
by Tricia Andryszewski.
p.   cm.—(Issue and debate)
Includes bibliographical references and index.
Summary: This book examines the history of
immigration to the United States and looks
specifically at both the positive and negative
effects recent newcomers have had on America.
ISBN 1-56294-499-1
1. United States—Emigration and immigration—History—Juvenile
literature.   2. United States—Emigration and immigration—Juvenile
literature.   I. Title.   II. Series.
JV6450.A65   1995
304.8'0973—dc20   94-21834   CIP   AC

Photographs courtesy of Gamma-Liaison: pp. 8 (Chip Hires),
20 (Anthony Suau); AP/Wide World: pp. 15, 65, 68, 73, 101;
Bettmann Archive: pp. 26, 30, 33; Brown Brothers: pp. 35, 38,
41; UPI/Bettmann: pp. 45, 55, 97; Rothco Cartoons: pp. 52
(Al Liederman), 78, (Dennis Renault, Sacramento *Bee*).

Published by The Millbrook Press
2 Old New Milford Road, Brookfield, Connecticut 06804

Contents

Immigration

Black, white, Latino, Asian—the high school students in this photo represent the many kinds of people who have immigrated to the United States. Just as varied have been the responses of established Americans to newcomers.

Two Centuries of Controversy About Immigrants

Americans have held conflicting views about immigration for hundreds of years, since before the American colonies became the United States. We haven't always been happy about welcoming newcomers:

> *Why should the [German] Palatine boors be suffered to swarm into our settlements and by herding together, establish their language and manners to the exclusion of ours? Why should Pennsylvania, founded by the English, become a colony of aliens, who will shortly be so numerous as to Germanize us, instead of our Anglifying them?*[1]   Benjamin Franklin, 1751

Yet we have gladly given millions refuge:

> *Every spot of the Old World is overrun with oppression. Freedom hath been hunted round the globe. Asia and Africa have long expelled her. Europe regards her as a stranger and England hath given her warning to depart. O! receive the*

fugitive and prepare in time an asylum for man-
kind.[2]   Thomas Paine, *Common Sense,* 1776

Hostility toward immigrants has been fueled by bigotry:

[Chinese immigrants] have never adapted them-
selves to our habits, mode of dress, or our edu-
cational system, have never learned the sanctity
of an oath, never desired to become citizens, or
to perform the duties of citizenship, never dis-
covered the difference between right and wrong,
never ceased the worship of their idol gods, or
advanced a step beyond the traditions of their
native hive.[3]   California State Legislature
report, 1876

Yet a generous welcome to immigrants is a proud part
of America's heritage:

Give me your tired, your poor,
Your huddled masses yearning to breathe free,
The wretched refuse of your teeming shore.
Send these, the homeless, tempest-tost to me:
I lift my lamp beside the golden door.[4]
Emma Lazarus, sonnet inscribed in 1903
at the base of the Statue of Liberty

We've taken advantage of cheap immigrant labor, yet
feared losing jobs to immigrants:

We condemn . . . the present system, which
opens up our ports to the pauper and criminal
classes of the world, and crowds out our wage
earners.[5]   People's Party platform, 1882

We've been the world's ethnic melting pot, but we worry about newcomers who don't blend in:

You can be born here [in Miami] in a Cuban hospital, be baptized by a Cuban priest, buy all your food from a Cuban grocer, take your insurance from a Cuban broker, and pay for it all with a check from a Cuban bank. You can get all the news in Spanish. You can go through life without having to speak English at all.[6]

Maurice A. Ferre,
mayor of Miami, 1986

We worry about running out of room:

If the United States should grow for the next two hundred years at the same rate we grew during the last two hundred years, there would be three times as many people in the United States than in the entire world today. Such a scenario is not only a nightmare—it is likely impossible. America, at some point, must stabilize its population.[7]

Richard D. Lamm,
governor of Colorado, 1992

And we worry about balancing immigration with the needs of people already living in America:

We can't afford to lose control of our borders [to illegal immigrants] or to take on new financial burdens at a time when we are not adequately providing for the jobs, the health care, and the education of our own people.[8]

President Bill Clinton, 1993

The United States was created by immigrants, yet it has often been hostile to newcomers. Established Americans at various times and places have welcomed, been indifferent to, or opposed immigration for many reasons, such as the state of the economy and how "different" a particular wave of newcomers seemed.

Over several hundred years, the mix of people the United States has attracted—and the choices we've made about who could enter—have shaped America's past and present. The people who choose and are allowed to come here now will help shape our future.

This book gathers together information that illuminates the debate about immigration, starting with a picture of who is migrating throughout the world today and why. Next comes an outline of the history of immigration to America and the controversies that came with it, followed by a look at immigration's economic impact and two especially contentious immigration issues—illegal immigration and asylum.

2
World Migration in the 1990s

Immigrants coming to America are part of a much larger worldwide pool of migrants (people who have left their homelands). The number of migrants, their reasons for migrating, and their characteristics (where they've come from, age, education level, etc.) change over time. A snapshot of today's migrants would look quite different from a similar picture taken ten or twenty years ago.

In recent years, the world has been awash in unprecedented numbers of migrants. Modern transportation, cheaper and more widely available than it has ever been, enables more people to migrate farther from their homelands. At the end of 1993, nearly 20 million refugees lived outside their native countries, most of them in developing nations. An additional 24 million were displaced from their homes inside the borders of their nations.[1] The World Bank estimated in 1992 that, altogether, world migrants—refugees, migrant workers and their families, and others—totaled 100 million.[2] Who are these migrants? Some are refugees from war or disaster. Some have migrated to find work. Some seek to settle permanently in a new country; others plan to return someday to their original homelands.

Increasingly, whole families migrate, not just individuals. In the 1960s and 1970s, male workers typically migrated alone, but by the 1980s many family members were following along. Today, worldwide, women and men migrate in nearly equal numbers, with most women in most regions migrating to find work—or to escape unbearable conditions at home—rather than simply to follow family.[3]

Converging Reasons for Migration. Policy makers in the United States and elsewhere try to draw sharp distinctions among those fleeing political oppression (entitled to asylum), refugees from natural disasters (deserving of humanitarian assistance), and migrating workers (liable to be shipped back whence they came). But developments around the world have blurred these distinctions and challenged us to come up with new ways to respond to migration.

Increasingly in many places, reasons for migration are converging and compelling great numbers of people to leave their homelands. Haiti—described here in the 1980s—is a vivid example of how complicated and urgent the reasons for mass migration can be:

Haiti, already the poorest country in the Western Hemisphere, also has the fastest-growing population. One third of the nation's land, exhausted by decades of deforestation and poor husbandry, is now virtually useless, and about 40 percent of the population is malnourished. More than half of the land is held by less

Two boys fight over a container of milk outside a looted Haitian supermarket. Wrenching poverty and political turmoil—the country's first democratically elected president was forced into exile in 1991—have driven scores of Haitians from their homeland.

*than 4 percent of the planters. The average holding for
a peasant farmer is less than an acre.*

*When food production per person began to decline
in the fifties, farmers began adding to their incomes by
selling charcoal. As trees vanished, so did the topsoil,
further reducing food production and increasing reli-
ance on charcoal for income. A combination of political
repression, economic decline, and environmental devastation has pushed an estimated one million refugees—
one sixth of Haiti's population—out of the country over
the past decades.*[4]

Jodi L. Jacobson
Worldwatch Institute, 1988

Is the typical Haitian migrant fleeing pervasive political
violence, a collapsed economy, or an overpopulated and
bankrupt natural environment? Probably all three.

Economic Migration. When an area's population
grows faster than its economy, people will leave in
search of work and a better life. This kind of migration
is not new. Over the past century and a half, for example, so many people have left Ireland for the United
States that there are far more people of Irish descent
living in the United States than in Ireland.

An unprecedented number of people around the
world are migrating today at least partly for economic
reasons. Over the past half century, income per person
in wealthier countries has tripled while it has remained
flat in poorer countries.[5] This has created a powerful
incentive for many people to migrate. The world's two
main magnets for economic migration in recent years
have been western Europe (which attracts migrants from southern and eastern Europe as well

as from northern Africa and the Middle East) and North America.

The United States attracts economic migrants from all over the world, but especially from Mexico. Not only does Mexico share a long border with the United States, but its economy offers workers compelling reasons to migrate: In the 1980s Mexican workers' productivity rose while wages *fell;* wages began to rise again in 1987, but by 1993 they still hadn't recovered even to 1980 levels.[6]

Demographic Pressures. World population is increasing fast: The number of people on this planet grows by about 90 million each year. During 1992 world population reached 5.5 billion, and it is expected to reach 10 billion before leveling off in the next century.[7]

This staggering population growth is concentrated in the less-developed areas of the world: Africa, Asia, and Latin America. Infant mortality has dropped considerably in even the poorest countries in this century, but birthrates in most of the developing world have not dropped so much, so the populations of these countries are disproportionately young. Even if these countries' birthrates drop, their populations will continue to grow for two or three generations, while all those young people—and their children—raise families.

In Mexico, for example, the average number of children born to each woman throughout her life had—by 1993—been falling for nearly a generation. But because of the higher birthrates of earlier years, the work force continued to grow by a million people a year. (In contrast, by the 1990s only two million new workers were being added each year in the United States, which has a population almost three times the size of Mexico's and an economy nearly thirty times as large.)[8] Rural and developing economies can't absorb all the young people entering the work force each year, so young people migrate in search of work—from rural areas to cities, and from less-developed regions to the developed economies of Europe and North America.

Rural-to-Urban Migration. Rural areas throughout the world have been experiencing changes—not all of them economic—that push people off farms and into cities. These changes include: population growing beyond what local farms can support; investment in large-scale agriculture that reduces the need for farm labor; a decline in opportunities and services in rural areas compared to cities; livelihoods derived from traditional grazing, fishing, forest, and other common rights being lost to private property interests; pollution and erosion cutting agricultural productivity.

By the early 1990s, 20 million to 30 million of the world's poorest people were migrating from rural to urban areas each year,[9] while the urban areas of the developing world couldn't provide enough services or economic opportunity to keep up with their growing populations. Millions of migrants leave these overflowing cities each year for countries that offer greater economic opportunities. Some have come to the United States; many more would like to.

Rural-to-urban migration is unevenly distributed around the world, and regional factors have a great impact on it. In Africa, for example, the widespread acquired immune deficiency syndrome (AIDS) epidemic tends to kill people in their most productive years. This has further weakened already fragile economies, families, and health and social security systems in the areas hit hardest and has spurred migration to cities.

In Latin America and Asia, rural-to-urban migration has slowed recently, and most urban growth now comes from children being born in the cities.[10] Nonetheless, the migration that has already taken place has been so massive (Mexico City, for example, grew from 3.5 million in 1950 to 18 million in 1992)[11] and the populations of the developing cities are so young that they will continue to grow rapidly for many years, even if rural migration slows to a trickle.

Environmental Pressures. Overpopulation and careless development cause or worsen many kinds of environmental damage: deforestation, soil erosion, desertification, and especially water contamination and shortages. These problems are not new: As long ago as 2500 to 2000 B.C., in the Middle East, powerful Sumerian city-states collapsed because centuries of intensive, unsustainable irrigated farming had destroyed the land's ability to feed a growing population.[12]

A stressed environment is more prone to catastrophe—and overpopulation pushes people into catastrophically risky situations. Draining wetlands and cutting forests make floods more extreme; more people living in a floodplain means more people left homeless when the floods come; houses built on deforested hillsides are vulnerable to disastrous mudslides.

Environmental degradation (damage that reduces an ecosystem's ability to support life) swells the number of migrants in many categories: victims of drought and other natural disasters made worse by previous human-caused damage, internal migrants who have exhausted the resources of one patch of land and must move to another, rural-to-urban migrants, refugees from civil conflicts aggravated by competition for ever-scarcer resources, and victims of technological disasters, such as

Migration to Mexico City became so massive during the late 1980s that satellite cities, where people with no other homes put up shacks, soon ringed the city. As this photo shows, such settlements often lacked basic facilities, such as sewers.

the tens of thousands forced to leave their homes in the area around the failed Soviet nuclear power plant at Chernobyl.[13] The number of such migrants that we see today may be much smaller than what we'll see in the future. Perhaps as many as 50 million refugees would be set adrift if global warming were to cause only a one-yard rise in the level of the world's oceans.[14]

Political Pressures. Political crises, by themselves or in combination with population pressures, economic incentives, and environmental degradation, can also generate waves of migrants—or close off migration routes, leaving large numbers with no place to go. Wars in Africa, Southeast Asia, and Central America have all set waves of migrants adrift in recent years. The 1990–1991 Gulf War uprooted perhaps two million migrants from Asia and various Arab states who had been working in Iraq and other Persian Gulf states.[15] And the collapse of the Soviet bloc and the disintegration of Yugoslavia have let loose a mass migration of millions toward western Europe.

The experiences of several refugees from the civil war in Somalia, who came to the United States in 1993, illustrate some of the difficulties experienced by even those war refugees lucky enough to find safe and stable new homes:

Transplanted from the bleak but familiar chaos of the refugee camps to an alien and often indecipherable city . . . they were greeted by strangers and left in a neighborhood [in Washington, D.C.] where they knew no one.

"That night I never forget," [Mohamad] Hussein said of his introduction to [his new home] in June,

*which marked the end of an odyssey that began 24
hours earlier in Kenya. "We don't know anything. I
open the door. They say, 'This is your home.' . . . They
give the key. They say, 'See you tomorrow.'*

*"How's up? How's down?" he said, trying to ex-
plain the disorientation he and his wife and nephew
felt. . . .*

*"We were so afraid. It was a dark night. . . . All
we are saying is Allah will save you. Maybe tomorrow." . . .*

*Like . . . most of the other Somali men, Hussein
was accepted as a refugee because he had worked at
the U.S. Embassy in Mogadishu. He spent seven months
in a refugee camp in Kenya, waiting for a chance to
emigrate and find what he vaguely hoped would be
a better life. His apartment, like that of other refugees,
is now furnished with castaway furniture. The bounty
includes an old crushed-velvet sofa and chairs and the
best curbside find yet, a 12-inch Goldstar television that
he and another family share. "Two nights here. Two
nights upstairs," Hussein said.*

*The need for money and services is a constant pre-
occupation. . . . Refugees get a stipend of about $5 a
day for the first three weeks, until emergency food
stamps are available. By the beginning of the second
month, they should receive a welfare check and regular
food stamps. They are then expected to pay a share of
the monthly rent. . . . After eight months, all federal
aid ends, and they are on their own.*[16]

The Washington Post
November 28, 1993

Where Do They Come From, Where Are They Going?

Many countries sheltering large numbers of refugees are
among the world's poorest; the refugees are often from

war-stricken neighboring countries. Thailand, for example, in 1991 hosted half a million refugees from Indochina and Myanmar (Burma); Pakistan and Iran took in six million Afghans in the 1980s; and in Africa, Malawi by the end of 1991 had accepted nearly a million refugees from neighboring Mozambique.[17]

A few Asian countries—Japan, South Korea, Singapore, Malaysia—have attracted migrant workers from other Asian countries to work in their expanding economies. (Some of these migrants stay longer than they're welcome: 280,000 foreigners overstayed their legally permitted visits in Japan in 1992, up from just 20,500 in 1989.)[18] Most Asian nations, though—especially the Philippines, countries in the Indian subcontinent, South Korea, and Vietnam—export large numbers of laborers to nations all over the world. The largest nation, China, restricts emigration but has the potential to unleash more migrants than any other nation:

The work force in China right now is about 580 million people, roughly 160 million of them in urban areas, and the rest in the countryside. But out of that 400-plus million in the countryside, less than 200 million are needed on the farm. And so they've got this surplus population in the countryside of 200 million, plus it is growing by 20 million per year. What do they do with these people? They've started rural industries that are doing very well but they absorb roughly a hundred million people. Okay. What do you do with the other 130, 140 million people? Well, what they've done is they have allowed them to drift towards the coast to the big cities looking for work." [19]

James McGregor
The Wall Street Journal
November 9, 1993

Of course, there's not enough work for these people in the cities either, and many seek ways to emigrate illegally.

In Africa, especially western Africa, a great deal of migration has traditionally taken place within particular regions, and this flow continues. But civil wars and war-caused famines have forced millions of additional Africans to migrate in recent years. Most of these migrants have remained in Africa. In southern Africa, migration along the established path to work in South Africa has decreased. But from northern Africa, record numbers in recent years have migrated to western Europe.

About 15 million migrants entered western Europe between 1980 and 1992.[20] Some were from Africa and Asia, and most recently huge numbers have migrated from the former Soviet Union and Warsaw Pact states and from the war-torn former Yugoslavia. Formerly Communist states in eastern and central Europe that have very little experience dealing with immigration are now receiving large numbers of migrants, from within their region as well as from developing nations.

Latin America sends many migrants abroad, and Mexico tops the list of the region's sending countries (Colombia is second). Virtually all of the migrants from Mexico go to the United States, legally or illegally.

The United States, of course, draws immigrants from all over the world. The mix and numbers of immigrants admitted to America have changed dramatically over the years—and so has the complex set of rules devised to regulate immigration.

3

Immigration Before the Twentieth Century

All of the people living in the United States are immigrants or descendants of immigrants. Even the American Indians met by the first European explorers were descended from immigrants to North America: Their ancestors had migrated from Asia before the most recent Ice Age ended about ten thousand years ago.

From Colonial Times to the Civil War. When we talk about American immigrants, we mean primarily those who have arrived during the past several hundred years. At first, they were mostly northern Europeans and slaves brought from Africa. Before the American Revolution, when the colonies were still under British rule, most immigrants—about three quarters of them—were British Protestants.

By the end of the colonial period, however, significant numbers of non-British settlers had also arrived. The largest number of these were German Protestants. Many settled in Pennsylvania, and among their descendants are today's Pennsylvania Dutch. Smaller numbers

An early wave of strangers to North America's shores: John Winthrop, center, led some seven hundred English immigrants to Massachusetts in 1630, hoping to establish a Puritan community.

of immigrants of other ethnic groups came as well: Catholic Irish, French Protestants (Huguenots), and Dutch, Swiss, Swedish, and Spanish settlers. In addition, perhaps half a million African slaves and another half a million American Indians lived in the newly independent United States. The nation's white population, by 1790, was something over three million.

We don't know just how many immigrants came to America in the early years. (Systematic records of immigration weren't kept before 1819, and truly comprehensive records weren't kept until the twentieth century). But it's clear that more and more kept coming—a quarter of a million between the end of the Revolutionary War and 1819, the U.S. Census Bureau believes.[1]

During those years, many longer-established residents demonstrated an anxiety that has recurred throughout American history: They became concerned that immigration was hurting the character of their society. Benjamin Franklin and others worried that German immigrants would overwhelm English-speaking Pennsylvania. Thomas Jefferson warned that unrestricted immigration would create "a heterogeneous, incoherent, distracted mass."[2] Anti-immigrant and anti-foreign attitudes were common, even among educated people.

Up to the time of the Civil War, most American anti-immigrant sentiment was also anti-Catholic. The United States was then an overwhelmingly Protestant society, and distaste for Catholicism had been carried over from Europe by most of America's earliest settlers.

In the 1830s, anti-foreign political parties emerged in several American cities and evolved into the strong nativist movement of the 1850s. ("Nativism" favors a country's native residents over immigrants.) The mid-1800s was a time of great upheaval in Europe, and the Irish potato famine as well as the failed revolts of 1848 brought large numbers of immigrants—a great many of them Catholic—to the United States. The anti-foreign, anti-Catholic "Americanists" who opposed this immigration built an organization called the Order of the Star-Spangled Banner; people who opposed the nativists called them the Know-Nothings.

The Know-Nothing movement didn't survive the Civil War—it couldn't be reconciled with two competing national loyalties (to the Confederacy and to the Union). Anxiety about immigrants, however, did survive. But its character changed as the ethnicity of America's immigrants changed.

First U.S. Immigration Restrictions. No federal laws restricted immigration throughout the first century after U.S. independence. In fact, immigration was a responsibility of the state governments until a series of Supreme Court decisions between 1849 and 1876 handed the matter over to Congress. The target of Congress's first restrictive actions on this issue was not, as might have been expected, the large number of Europeans migrating across the Atlantic. It was the smaller but still substantial flow of Chinese immigrants to California.

The Gold Rush of 1849 first attracted large numbers of Chinese workers to California, where they did a great deal of mostly menial work for very low pay. Many Chinese immigrants worked on the construction of the transcontinental railroad, which was completed in 1869:

More than ten thousand Chinese were recruited or especially imported to lay the track for the Central Pacific Railroad that was being built eastward from Sacramento in the late sixties in furious competition with the Union Pacific, which had gangs of Irish laborers working west from Omaha. . . .

The difficulties were enormous, particularly in the Sierra peaks in the winter, where snowsheds had to be built to keep the tracks from being buried. Drilling through granite to bore a tunnel at the summit, the workers progressed less than a foot a day, but during the final spurt—six years after the first construction had begun—when they were rushing toward Salt Lake City to meet the Union Pacific, they were averaging a mile of track a day. . . .

The Chinese brought their own cooks and performed this feat of building a railroad across some of the world's most formidable obstacles on a diet chiefly of dried fish, rice, and tea. They also used some of their own equipment and methods, such as hanging from wicker baskets to chip ledges in the sheer vertical cliffs, and carrying the black powder used for blasting between bamboo poles. Many lost their lives in explosions of nitroglycerin; others died of over-exertion. As some fell by the wayside, temporarily or permanently, the contractors made sure that there was a sufficient labor pool so that another crew would be ready for the next shift. [3]

Anne Loftis, *California—*
Where the Twain Did Meet

In the 1870s, the Gold Rush ended. Large numbers of European immigrants and native-born Americans from the East began to make their way to California, and the region's economy stalled. Tough competition for work mixed with racial prejudice to foster growing hostility toward the Chinese immigrants.

In 1882, Congress prohibited the immigration of any more Chinese laborers. (They also barred such other "excludables" as lunatics, prostitutes, convicts, and anyone likely to become dependent on public financial support.) In 1888, Congress prohibited Chinese workers already in the United States from returning if they should ever leave the country, however briefly, and in 1892 the

This cartoon shows the many "bricks" that built the anti-Chinese "wall" in 1882, when Congress prohibited the immigration of Chinese workers.

lawmakers authorized forcing some Chinese in the United States to return to China. Statute by statute, more restrictions were added. Immigration from other Asian states was also retricted; President Theodore Roosevelt's 1906 "Gentlemen's Agreement" with the Japanese government, for example, curtailed immigration from Japan. By 1917 the list of excludables included virtually anyone born in Asia.

Mid-1800s to 1920s. But Asians were only a small part of America's rapidly changing immigration picture. The foreign-born population of the United States in 1850 totaled about 2.24 million. Of these, 1.44 million were from northern and western Europe—and of these, nearly 1 million were English-speaking Irish. Only somewhat more than half a million (almost all German) of America's foreign-born were from central and eastern Europe. And only a scant eight thousand immigrants had come from the Mediterranean states of southern Europe.[4]

By about 1880, dramatic changes were under way: Great numbers of immigrants were for the first time able to come to America from southern and eastern Europe. Most of these newcomers didn't speak English; their cultures were Latin and Slavic; and their religious affiliations were Catholic, Orthodox, and Jewish. Altogether, they seemed more "foreign" than the mostly northern European, mostly Protestant immigrants of earlier times.

Census data reveal just how much the ethnicity of America's immigrants had changed. The number of those living in America who had been born in Ireland doubled, to nearly 1.9 million, between 1850 and 1890—but the number of Irish entering the country each year stopped growing by around 1870.[5]

The number of those living in America who had been born in central and eastern Europe multiplied *six times* between 1850 and 1890, and nearly doubled again between 1890 and 1910. As late as 1890, these were still mostly Germans, but so many Slavs were entering the country by then that by 1910 there were more of them living here than Germans.[6]

Immigrants from southern Europe had totaled just eight thousand in 1850. By 1890, more than 200,000 had arrived. This number more than doubled in ten years (to more than half a million by 1900), then *tripled* again in the next decade, to 1.5 million by 1910. Southern European immigrants were not a large fraction of the total foreign-born population, which reached 13.3 million in 1910, but their numbers were growing stunningly fast.[7] As late as the 1880s, one quarter of all arriving immigrants spoke German; by 1901–1910, almost one quarter of those arriving spoke Italian.[8]

Not only was the ethnic composition of America's immigrants changing dramatically, but unprecedented numbers of them were arriving as well. Between 1890 and 1914, more than 16 million arrived, 1.3 million in 1907 alone. At the turn of the century, fully one third of New York City's 3.5 million residents were foreign-born. (Especially large numbers of new immigrants settled in the cities in New York, Pennsylvania, Massachusetts, Illinois, and New Jersey.) Overall, by 1910, nearly 15 percent of America's population was foreign-born.[9]

Ellis Island. Many of these immigrants—more than 12 million—passed through one gateway: Ellis Island, in New York Harbor, near the Statue of Liberty. Before 1890, each state government had been responsible for administering immigration. After the federal government took over this responsibility, it opened Ellis Island in 1892 as its first official inspection station. Between 1892 and 1924 more than half of all immigrants entering the United States passed through Ellis Island.[10]

One of these immigrants—one of the hundreds of thousands who fled Europe in the wake of World War I—was twenty-one-year-old Bronislawa Tanajewski, who arrived at Ellis Island in 1920. Blanche (as she came to be called in America) and her mother had left their home in Souvalki, a small town in rural eastern

This 1911 photo shows immigrant children being checked at Ellis Island for, among other diseases, typhus, which was responsible for millions of deaths around the world at that time.

Poland, in early spring of 1920. Their story is typical of immigrants of that time, but—like every immigrant's story—it is also unique.

From the beginning, things didn't go according to plan, but they were very anxious to leave and made the best of their circumstances. Blanche's father had planned to come with them, but he was too sick to make the journey. He told Blanche and her mother he'd join them later in America. He never made it.

Blanche traveled alone to Warsaw to collect money for the journey that had been sent by relatives already living in America. She returned home, then she and her mother traveled from Souvalki to the American consulate in Warsaw, where they got documents giving them permission to enter America. They then traveled north to the port city of Danzig (now known as Gdansk), where Blanche bought their tickets for passage on a boat to New York.

Months went by while the agents Blanche bought the tickets from promised that their boat would arrive "in a few days." Finally, in August, Blanche and her mother boarded a boat for America. They had little luggage. Earlier, thinking that her mother had packed too much (including goose-down pillows—her mother didn't think there were suitable geese in America), Blanche "lost" some baggage off the side of a train.

Before they were allowed on the boat, kerosene was poured over their heads to kill any lice they might have brought. When they finally boarded the boat, they discovered it had been used to transport cattle—and hadn't been converted to carry passengers. Blanche and her mother shared a stall, its floor covered with straw, during the three-week journey across the Atlantic Ocean.

When they finally arrived at New York Harbor, U.S. immigration officials took down their names, then required them to hand over all their clothes and take

Immigrants were also given intelligence tests at Ellis Island. Here a woman is required to match shapes with spaces.

disinfectant showers. Blanche handed over her nice traveling dress; when she got it back, disinfected, it was a wrinkled mess.

Blanche and her mother stayed on Ellis Island for three days, in quarantine (isolated to make sure they didn't carry infectious diseases into the country), sleeping on cots in a large open room. Compared to their gruesome ocean voyage, it made Blanche feel as if "we came into heaven." They spoke no English. When the quarantine was completed, relatives (including Blanche's sister) took Blanche and her mother to live with them in Jersey City, New Jersey.

A few days later, Blanche got her first real look at New York City, just across the river from her new home, when one of her relatives took her to Delancy Street. All she noticed were hundreds of pushcarts, laundry hanging off tenement fire escapes, and a big, ugly elevated train running down the middle of the street.

She cried. She had left a young man she was supposed to marry back in Souvalki because she thought "the gold was going to fall from the trees" in America, and she would "just pick it up." When they returned to Jersey City, Blanche told her mother that she was going to go back to Europe.

In the days ahead, Blanche saw more of New York. She saw the high-rises on Broadway, the mansions along Fifth Avenue—and she saw that America wasn't so bad after all. She decided to stay.[11]

Although the mass processing of immigrants at Ellis Island ended in 1924, by then it had seen a large proportion of our population pass through its gates. Even today, more than seventy years later, as many as 40 percent of Americans have ancestors who first arrived at Ellis Island.

4

Narrowing the Gate: Twentieth-Century Immigration

The arrival of so many immigrants once again stirred anti-immigrant anxiety in America. By the 1920s, however, the character of American nativism had changed from what it had been during the heyday of the Know-Nothings. Anti-Catholic bigotry was less widespread. The greater fears by the 1920s were that foreigners would render America unrecognizable by changing its ethnic mix or would subvert the nation with political radicalism.

Fear of radical political activity had always colored Americans' attitudes toward foreigners. Although many Americans (sons and daughters of the American Revolution) cheered on popular revolts in Europe and elsewhere, many also feared that radical ideas from other nations might bring chaos to America. Sometimes these fears shaped public policy: As early as 1798 to 1801, the Alien and Sedition Acts allowed the federal government to deport "subversive" foreigners.

*As armed citizens look on from their
cars, some 1,200 members of the Indus-
trial Workers of the World, an organization
suspected of Communist ties, are rounded up
and marched into custody. This photo
was taken in 1917 during the Red Scare,
when fear of communism contributed to
American uneasiness over newcomers.*

Fear of foreign radicalism increased after the failed European revolutions of 1848. German immigrants founded a Marxist movement in America, the growing U.S. trade union movement maintained ties to international socialism, and anarchists (many of them foreign-born) preached that all government should be abolished. This worldwide surge of political radicalism—and America's anxious reaction to it—peaked in the Russian Revolution of 1917 and the U.S. Red Scare of the 1920s.

Fear of the Red Menace intensified widespread doubts about the wisdom of allowing so much immigration and fueled anxiety about America's changing ethnic mix. Fearing revolution, officials added to the list of reasons for exclusion from immigration. By 1917, this list included not only political radicals but also polygamists (who believed that God permitted men to have several wives) and people with contagious tuberculosis. Dealing with the ethnic question, however, required more than just tinkering with the list of excludables. The issue inspired a wholesale overhaul of America's immigration system.

The Quota System. In the 1920s, Congress passed a series of laws creating an immigration quota system designed to freeze the proportions of people of various ethnic heritages living in the United States. For the first time, a limit was set on the total number of people who could immigrate each year. This quota, intentionally set very low, hovered around 150,000, not including immigrating spouses and children of U.S. citizens, who were automatically eligible for admission.

The quota was assigned country by country in numbers matching the proportion that each ethnic group had made up in the U.S. population in 1890—before most of the eastern and southern Europeans had arrived. The vast majority of entry visas (permissions to enter the country) were thus set aside for immigrants from the British Isles and Germany. Immigration from southern and eastern Europe was severely limited; Asians and Africans were virtually excluded. (The quota system did not apply to immigration from Canada or Latin America, which remained unrestricted, except for health, moral, and political exclusions.)

Immigration dropped sharply, and it remained low for decades. During the 1930s Depression and World War II, immigration sank below even the low levels specified by the quotas. (In several of these years, more people left the country than came in.) The quota system was tragically inflexible for Jews trying to flee Nazi persecution in the late 1930s. U.S. politicians were reluctant to raise any immigrant quotas while millions of Americans remained unemployed as a result of the Depression. Many thousands of Jews who were refused safe haven in the United States later died in Nazi concentration camps.

The 1920s quota system remained in place for four decades, although Congress did tinker with it from time to time. The McCarran-Walter Act of 1952, for example, lengthened the list of reasons for exclusion in response to a new Red Scare sweeping the country. McCarran-Walter also specified that, within the limits of the national quotas, half of the visas be allocated to people with urgently needed skills and half to relatives of U.S. residents.

The quota system worked less and less well as the century wore on. Increasing numbers of immigrants were admitted under exceptions to the system that were occasionally specified by Congress. And, as Europe's

While it reduced immigration to the United States, the Depression displaced many Americans. This photo shows a "Hooverville," a community of makeshift homes named for the U.S. president during whose administration the stock market crashed.

economy grew robustly after World War II, fewer of its people wished to emigrate, so some of the U.S. immigration quotas allocated to European countries went unfilled. For example, by the early 1960s the annual quota for the United Kingdom was 65,000—but on average only about 28,000 actually came to America.[1]

1965 to 1990. The immigration system was clearly due for a complete overhaul. When it got one, in 1965, President Lyndon B. Johnson said that the new legislation "repair[ed] a deep and painful flaw in the fabric of American justice"[2] by abolishing the national quota system for immigration. No longer would an unchanging ethnic mix be the goal of U.S. immigration policy; instead, family reunification became its chief objective.

The revised system permitted 270,000 immigrants to enter each year, with no more than 20,000 to come from any one country. (An additional 120,000 Canadians and Latin Americans were permitted entry outside this system; it wasn't until 1976 that these nations were. brought under the same set of rules that governed immigration from the rest of the world.) Most of the annual entry visas were reserved for close relatives of U.S. residents. Spouses, parents, and minor children of U.S. citizens didn't have to compete for these visas, since they automatically qualified for immigration outside the 270,000 limit.

The number of immigrants now rose. But not only did the number rise—the ethnic mix changed as well. The 1920s immigration restrictions had effectively frozen out Asian and African immigrants. After 1965, the change in U.S. policy and changes in international conditions caused the number of immigrants from developing countries to soar, reaching about 90 percent of total admissions by the late 1980s.[3] In 1965 more than half of U.S. immigrants had come from Europe and Canada; since then, most new arrivals have come from Asia and Latin America, with the largest number coming from Mexico—legally and, in increasing numbers, illegally.[4]

Fear that the United States had lost control of its southern border led to enactment of the Immigration Reform and Control Act of 1986 (IRCA). For the first time in U.S. history, employers were to be penalized for hiring illegal immigrants. IRCA also gave legal status to immigrants who had lived in the United States illegally since before 1982, as well as a large number of farm workers. Altogether, close to three million illegal immigrants were granted amnesty—forgiveness for entering the country illegally, and legal permission to stay—under IRCA.

In 1990, Congress made additional changes to the immigration system. According to these changes, by 1995, 675,000 immigrants were to be admitted annually, most of them under family-unification provisions. Smaller numbers would be admitted on skill-based visas and "diversity" visas designed to boost immigration from countries that had in the past sent few migrants to America. Congress in 1990 also defined several categories of workers who were to be allowed temporary residence, and it revised the list of reasons for exclusion, dictating that no one be denied entry solely because of political beliefs and limiting health exclusions to those posing a public health risk. (Other reasons for exclusion screen out criminals, people unable to support themselves, and national security risks.)[5]

Many immigration and human-rights activists hoped that these changes would lead to a lifting of the ban, in place since 1987, on visitors infected with the human immunodeficiency virus (HIV). But, as of mid-1994, the ban remained in place. Supporters of the ban said infected immigrants could spread AIDS among Americans and could become expensive burdens on the health care system. Critics point out that AIDS is not contagious through casual contact, that HIV-infected immigrants would be very few compared with the number of Americans already infected, that the exclusion inhumanely prevents family unification, and that even without the HIV ban immigration law allows exclusion of anyone likely to be a public economic burden.

The economic-burden exclusion has not been applied for health reasons in the past. Using it to exclude people with AIDS would raise a question of fairness: Should would-be immigrants who have—or who are likely to develop—other expensive medical conditions, such as cancer or liver failure, also be excluded?

Impact of Family-Unification Immigration. The 1990 legislation did not change a key component of U.S. immigration policy: Spouses, parents, and minor children of U.S. citizens remained eligible to immigrate, exempt from any numerical limit, provided they didn't fit any of the law's grounds for exclusion.

Family unification has probably benefited not only the families immediately affected but also the rest of us. Surprisingly, immigrants who join family members in the United States are on average better educated and more skilled than the family members who preceded them. It may well be that—instead of sending their best and brightest—families abroad are more willing to part with their *least* successful members, sending them on a sort of gamble to make their fortunes in America.[6]

Some people worry that the family-unification provisions build into our immigration policy the potential for explosive growth in immigration, as each immigrant

A Cuban immigrant greets a newly arrived relative in Miami, Florida. While some people worry that allowing family members to join immigrants will contribute to runaway population growth in the United States, others say it helps America: Family immigration tends to bring in more skilled newcomers.

sponsors his or her immediate family members, who in turn sponsor additional members of the family, who sponsor still more. So far, this doesn't seem to be happening, most likely for several reasons: Immigrants are not immediately eligible to sponsor relatives (it takes several years of U.S. residence). Not all family members *want* to come to the United States. And substantial numbers of immigrants plan to return to their homelands eventually, rather than bring their families here. (Of those who came here in the 1960s and 1970s, perhaps as many as one third have returned home.)[7]

But family-chain immigration may well increase if our policy remains open to it. It is a pattern more typical of immigration from less-developed countries, and as the proportion of immigrants from these countries has been increasing, so perhaps will future family-chain immigration.

Immigration Today. By the early 1990s, about one million immigrants were being added to the U.S. population each year, including perhaps 200,000 to 250,000 illegal immigrants. For the year ending in September 1993, the total number of immigrants granted legal permanent residence was 810,635, the largest number of whom were spouses, young children, and parents of adult U.S. citizens (235,484); other relatives sponsored under family-preference categories (213,123); workers granted special preferences (116,198); and refugees and asylees (117,037), a category that will be discussed in a separate chapter.[8]

The procedure a would-be immigrant follows to get into the United States depends on who he or she is. Spouses, young children, and parents of adult U.S. citizens have the easiest time of it: Once the State Department determines that they don't fit any of the law's criteria for automatic exclusion, these close relatives are immediately given permission to enter the United States and green cards certifying that they're legal permanent residents. Five years later, they're eligible to apply for U.S. citizenship. (A few other, much smaller categories of immigrants also enter the country under similar unrestrictive rules—Amerasians born in Vietnam, for example.)

Other would-be immigrants—if they're qualified in specific preference categories outlined by the law—can apply to enter the country under a more tightly restricted procedure. Limited numbers of less-immediate relatives are admitted each year under a family-preference system: Unmarried adult sons and daughters of U.S. citizens get first preference, spouses and unmarried sons and daughters of legal permanent residents get second preference, married sons and daughters of U.S. citizens are third, and brothers and sisters of adult U.S. citizens are fourth. Only 226,000 visas are issued each year for these less-immediate relatives, although many, many more people apply. A similar system issues 140,000 visas each year to five preference categories of workers who are highly trained or who have special skills.

People who apply under these numerically limited preference systems are first cleared by the State Department, then put on a waiting list. Separate waiting lists are kept for each preference category (sons go on a different list from brothers, for example)—and a separate set of waiting lists is kept for each foreign country, since the number of immigrants who can come from each country is also limited. The length of time a would-be immigrant has to wait varies, depending on his or her nationality and preference category. Most people who qualify for the worker-preference categories are granted visas quickly; some lower-preference relatives have been on waiting lists for twelve years or more. Applicants who reach the top of their list are given permission to enter the United States and green cards certifying that they're legal permanent residents. They may apply for U.S. citizenship after five years.

Altogether, about nine million legal and probably three million illegal immigrants arrived between 1983 and 1993.[9] These numbers were high, but fairly stable. (Studies showing a sharp upturn in the late 1980s and early 1990s included the three million immigrants granted legal permanent residence under IRCA. Most of these migrants had actually entered the country, though illegally, not in the late 1980s but years earlier.)

Who are these immigrants? Profiles of immigrants in and around Washington, D.C., indicate their diversity—and the hard lives many of them lead:

Maryam Zaidi's mornings begin in the dark, when she hauls herself out of bed to deliver 350 newspapers. . . . Her days end near midnight, after she leaves her job as a shop clerk . . . and helps her sister with homework. . . . During the daylight hours between jobs . . . [Zaidi, a native of India, attends college], studying calculus, computer science, and physics. . . . She works seven days a week . . . helps support her younger brother and two sisters, studies at all hours and maintains an 'A' average. Sometimes she even manages to get more than four hours of sleep a night.[10]

Cristina Farias is a nanny for a couple in Northwest Washington. She watches over two small children, does small household chores and, between the job and her commute from suburban Maryland, regularly puts in 12-hour days. In her native Chile, Farias was a college-educated accountant for a bank. Now . . . she makes

$360 a week, hoping that the computer course she is taking will one day help her land a job as a receptionist or secretary.

Tesfamariam Kidane . . . emigrated from Eritrea twenty years ago. . . . With a graduate degree in music, Kidane hoped to land a job teaching at a university when he moved to the Washington area seven years ago. But those dreams never panned out, and so Kidane makes a modest living juggling three jobs: picking up gigs with a local band, giving music lessons to a few private students and working as a bookkeeper three nights a week.

An immigrant from Peru, William Onofre arrived in Washington five years ago, speaking little English and possessing few skills that quickly could lead to professional employment. His first job was at a [pharmacy], where he mopped floors and stocked shelves for $3.75 an hour. Once his English improved through college courses, Onofre landed a job receiving packages for [a hotel] and doubled his salary in the process. Now, Onofre has an office job at the hotel, handling payroll, wearing a suit and tie to work.[11]

Washington Post
October 11 and July 5, 1993

One out of twelve U.S. residents in 1993 was foreign-born; in 1970 the figure was only one in twenty. But although the absolute number of recent immigrants surpasses even the great wave of European immigration at the beginning of this century, in proportion to the nation's population the rate of immigration now is only about one third of what it was then. Yesterday's newcomers made up a much greater part of the population: From 1860 to 1920, roughly one in seven U.S. residents was foreign-born.[12]

The impact of today's newcomers, however, is concentrated in just a few regions. Fully one third of all foreign-born residents in the United States today live in California; 75 percent of those who immigrated during the 1980s live in seven states.[13] And large ethnic groups of immigrants have clustered together in several areas: Asians in California, Latin Americans—especially Mexicans—in California and Texas, Cubans and Haitians in Miami, and large groups of many ethnicities in and around New York City. Immigrants throughout our history have concentrated in enclaves (areas dominated by particular ethnic groups), of course, creating the Chinatowns, Little Italys, barrios, and Polish districts of America's older cities.

In the difficult economy of the early 1990s, many people who favor reducing immigration fear that immigrants take jobs away from established Americans. The record numbers, high visibility, and unprecedented diversity of today's immigrants seem to have set off a strong new wave of American nativism.

Do immigrants really take jobs from native-born Americans, as many fear? What is the economic impact of immigration, now and historically, and how might it shape our future?

5

Immigrants and the U.S. Economy

Immigrants are commonly accused, now as in the past, of taking jobs away from native-born Americans and, by accepting lower wages, keeping everyone's wages low. But it's also widely believed that immigrants benefit America economically by taking jobs that established residents don't want, especially in such low-paying fields as child care, housekeeping, and agriculture.

Fear of the economic impact of immigration increases during times when Americans are worried about their own opportunities to make a living. In 1993, after years of recession and at a time when unemployment remained high, polls showed that two thirds of Americans wanted immigration to be reduced. Among those who were "very worried" about their economic situation, three quarters wanted less immigration. More than half of all who were polled thought government services to immigrants cost taxpayers too much, and only one third believed that immigrants eventually would become productive citizens who paid their share of taxes.[1]

As this cartoon suggests, in tough economic times, some Americans believe that immigrants will steal their jobs.

Economic Impact of Earlier Immigrants. Attitudes haven't always been this negative, and immigration has played a crucial role in America's economic development. In the earliest days, sparsely populated America was desperate for labor and welcomed whoever was willing to come work. From the mid-1800s to the early 1900s, immigrant labor fueled America's industrialization.

Not all immigrants became factory workers. Immigrants found work at all sorts of places, from sweatshops to farms to construction sites.

No matter which line of work they entered, most immigrant workers of the nineteenth and early twentieth centuries found life in America better than it was in the Old World. But they generally earned less than native-born Americans and didn't catch up to American wage levels in the immigrant generation's lifetime. Working their way up the economic ladder to a more comfortable lifestyle remained a dream to be realized by their children.[2]

From the 1920s to the 1960s—the decades of tightly restricted immigration—the economic impact of immigration was reduced along with the number of immigrants. In the 1950s, for example, immigration contributed only 17 percent of the growth in America's labor force (the rest came from native-born Americans growing up and entering the workplace).[3]

Even for a while after immigration increased again, in the 1970s, immigrants accounted for maybe as little as 11 percent of labor force growth, because two much larger groups entered the American work force during the same period: baby boomers (the very large generation born in the decade or so after World War II) and women. In 1960, only 38 percent of American women worked outside the home; by 1980, 52 percent did.[4] (Since then, this percentage has leveled off in the upper fifties.)[5]

Good data are lacking on the economic impact of earlier waves of immigrants, but economists believe that the 1970s immigrants—illegal as well as legal—had no significant effect on the wages or unemployment rates of native-born workers. The newcomers did, however, depress wages somewhat for the immigrants who preceded them, probably because they were competing most directly for the same work.[6]

In the 1980s and 1990s, the number of immigrants entering the United States rose, and so did the immigrant share of workers added to the labor force. (The U.S. Department of Labor estimates that immigrants accounted for 22 percent of new workers in the 1980s.)[7] Not only has the number of immigrants grown in recent years, but several economically significant characteristics of the immigrant population have changed.

A Changing Population of Immigrants. America attracts a mixed bag of immigrants, with increasing numbers coming from less-developed parts of the world. Since many groups of today's immigrants are at least as much different from each other as they are from native-born Americans, their experience of America is mixed as well.

Many economists believe that the post-1965 immigrants are on balance less skilled and therefore do less well in the work force than native-born Americans or earlier immigrants. The new immigrants do, on average, have higher unemployment rates and work fewer hours per year.[8]

The most critical factors for immigrants trying to make it in America are the number of years of schooling completed, English fluency, and experience living in a developed economy. Better-educated immigrants earn more per hour and work more hours per year than less-educated immigrants. (American employers generally, however, value foreign schooling less than a comparable U.S. education.)[9]

Immigrants also do better economically as they assimilate (learn how to fit in, to cope with American customs). The longer they're here, the better they tend to do. But other factors also influence how well and how quickly newcomers adjust. Immigrants who come from economic systems similar to ours have an obvious advantage for assimilating, and their wages catch up with those of natives more quickly than do those of other

An image of modern immigrant success: Duc Nguyen, a Vietnamese refugee, stacks goods in his grocery store, one of the many businesses he owns, including a restaurant, tailor shop, and video rental. He earned $2.80 an hour in his first job in the United States.

immigrants. And immigrants who know they can't go back—such as those who have fled political repression—also assimilate faster.[10]

Immigrants coming from some countries (Germany and Japan are two examples) do especially well in the United States. The wide differences in economic success among various national groups correspond very closely to differences in the immigrant groups' average skill levels: The average skill levels of immigrants from particular nations usually match the average skill levels of workers who stayed behind, but not always. Some nations send us disproportionate numbers of their college graduates, and others send more of their less-skilled workers.[11]

Further complicating the picture of who does how well in America, many immigrants eventually return to their homelands—perhaps as many as one quarter to one third of them. Some return as wealthy heroes, some as economic failures. Undoubtedly more return to some nations than to others, but changing international political and economic conditions make it difficult to predict which nations will be which.

New Immigrants and the U.S. Economy. More than any other factor, it's the state of the American economy that shapes how well immigrants fare in the United States. In boom times, skilled and unskilled workers fuel an expanding economy. But hard times in the American economy are especially hard on less-skilled workers, and disproportionate numbers of today's immigrants fall into this category. When unemployment is high, immigrant unemployment is especially high.

Recent immigration appears not to have decreased the wages or increased the unemployment rates of native-born Americans—not even in most areas that have absorbed high numbers of immigrants. However, workers in some regions (parts of California, especially) that have been hit hard by recession in the 1990s and have absorbed huge numbers of recent immigrants may be suffering from the immigrant competition. Some economists believe that such an effect is unavoidable in these circumstances, but the evidence about this is still inconclusive.

Some—but not all—native-born workers even seem to have benefited from the influx of immigrants in the 1980s: The wages of native-born white and Hispanic workers increased more in areas with high concentrations of immigrants than they did in other areas; however, wages of black workers in high-immigration areas remained flat. Now as in the past, the only workers likely to see wages drop as a result of immigration are immigrants who arrived earlier. Typically, a 10 percent increase in immigration causes foreign-born workers' wages to drop by at least 2 percent.[12]

Beyond wages and unemployment, the overall economic impact of accepting large numbers of less-skilled immigrants is likely to be mixed. On one hand, the cheap labor supplied by such immigrants lowers the production costs of some goods (in agriculture especially), and this may mean lower prices for U.S. consumers. On the other hand, less-skilled, lower-income workers pay less in taxes, add less wealth to America's economy, and use more government services than higher-income workers.

In the long run, the U.S. economy benefits from immigration, but in the short term accepting immigrants can be expensive. Arriving immigrants immediately need services ranging from health care to a share of expanded police protection and trash collection. But they also contribute human capital and taxes to our economy—benefits that take time to develop. As immigrants assimilate, their economic contribution grows.[13]

Health, Education, and Welfare. It's hard to calculate whether immigrants as a group "pay their way" in taxes for their share of government expenditures, but it seems likely that they do. At worst, any government spending beyond what immigrants pay in taxes is a very small piece of total U.S. social spending—although it's a very large piece of the budget in some states (California and Florida, especially) where recent immigrants are concentrated. Nonetheless, even if today's immigrants pay their way overall, it's likely that a different mix of immigrants—more skilled, with higher incomes—would pay more.

It's generally agreed—and required by federal law—that public education and emergency health care should be provided to everyone living in the United States, legal and illegal immigrants as well as natives. Some state and local laws require that at least some non-emergency health services be available to all in need, whether or not they can afford to pay.

How we should pay for these services is controversial. Public spending on health and education is divided among federal, state, and local governments, and the federal government has been picking up a smaller share of the bill in recent years. For example, federal funding for bilingual education (a service often required by immigrants' children) has decreased as immigration has increased, so that bilingual education services were, by 1993, available to fewer than 310,000 of the perhaps 2.3 million children who spoke limited English.[14]

Immigrants' use of other welfare services is also controversial. Except for refugees and asylees (immigrants who are seeking or have been granted asylum—

a safe haven in the United States away from persecution), who immediately qualify for various support services, immigrants aren't permitted to participate in most welfare programs until they've been in this country for several years. But permitted or not, some immigrants do slip into the welfare system, which is mostly locally administered and often not very efficient.

Welfare participation rates in recent years for immigrants as a group—recent as well as longer-established immigrants—have been only slightly higher than the welfare rates of native-born Americans. But this gap *increases* the longer immigrants are in the United States (partly because immigrants only become eligible for most programs after they've been here a while), unlike the differences between native and immigrant unemployment and wages, which decrease over time. Not all immigrant nationalities have higher-than-native welfare rates, but some (Mexicans, for example) have much higher rates than others. The different welfare rates of immigrants and native-born Americans are probably due to demographic differences: Immigrant families have on average less schooling and include disproportionate numbers of young children and the elderly, and all of these characteristics are associated with greater use of the welfare system.[15]

Some people worry that large numbers of immigrants come to the United States to exploit our welfare system, but that doesn't seem to be the case. Immigrants come here hoping to work and be successful. But even if they fail, many of the world's poor and less-skilled migrants will probably be better off here than they were in their native countries. Our welfare and social security system, adequate or not by our standards, may make it seem less risky for many to come to America.

Regional Impact of New Immigrants. Immigrants pay most of their taxes to the federal government but require many services—education, police protection, and some health and welfare services—that are funded locally or by state governments. So some states and cities where immigrants cluster find that immigration costs them a great deal.

Immigration and native-born population growth alike are concentrated in America's coastal regions, so immigration aggravates regional overcrowding and environmental problems, especially in Florida and coastal California. More of the recent immigrants live in the West than in the East; many of these have come from Mexico and Asia. And most live in cities: Our twenty-five largest metropolitan areas house only two fifths of native-born residents, but more than three quarters of immigrants. Six states—California, New York, Texas, Florida, Illinois, and New Jersey—hold two thirds of all immigrants but only one third of America's native-born population.[16]

Because immigration is concentrated in a few areas, a small overall increase in the number of immigrants coming to the United States—say, 10 percent—can as much as double the immigrant population in a few cities.[17] This can strain a local economy, especially if the increase is sudden, as it was in Miami after the 1980 Mariel boatlift, when more than 100,000 people arrived suddenly from Cuba. Large numbers of incoming immigrants not only stretch local social services thin but also may set off migrations of native-born Americans: Between 1985 and 1990, tens of thousands of low-income native-born Americans migrated *out* of states such as New York, Texas, and California where huge numbers of immigrants had recently moved in.[18]

Many proposals have been put forward in response to problems related to immigration. A lot of people would like to see some costs now paid locally shifted to the federal government. (California taxpayers, especially, seek relief. Their state is paying more for immigrant-related services than any other state at a time when its economy is weak.) Some activists have even suggested a complete national moratorium—a freeze—on immigration. But the most controversial ideas have been directed at the part of the problem that gets the most public attention: what to do about illegal immigration.

6

Illegal Immigration

A 1993 poll indicated that 68 percent of Americans believe that "most of the people who have moved to the United States in the last few years are here illegally."[1] They were wrong. Nearly nine million immigrated legally during the 1980s; in the same decade, perhaps three million settled here illegally.

It's hard to determine just how many people are here illegally, for the obvious reason that illegals seek to avoid detection. Different ways of calculating the number of illegal immigrants present various problems. For example, if we try to derive such a total from the number of illegals caught and turned back at the border (more than one million in 1992), we have to take into account that changes in this number are tied to changes in the Border Patrol budget, that many are seasonal workers who plan to stay in the United States only temporarily, and that many of those caught (and not caught) are repeaters.

Reasonable estimates of the number of illegal immigrants living in this country in 1993 range from 1.7 million to 5.5 million, according to the General Accounting Office (GAO) of the federal government. The GAO believes there are 3.4 million.[2] The Immigration and Naturalization Service (INS) estimates that 3.2 million were here illegally in 1992, up from 2.6 million in 1990.[3] The Census Bureau in 1993 guessed 4 million, growing by about 200,000 to 250,000 each year.[4] The total number of immigrants—legal and illegal—living here is probably about 20 million,[5] part of a total U.S. population of about 260 million.

A large population of illegal immigrants is obviously most unfair to the many thousands waiting at the gate who have applied for *legal* admission and been put on years-long waiting lists. But illegal immigration creates problems for citizens and legal residents, too.

On July 27, 1993, President Bill Clinton announced steps to curb illegal immigration:

We must not—and we will not—surrender our borders to those who wish to exploit our history of compassion and justice. We cannot tolerate those who traffic in human cargo, nor can we allow our people to be endangered by those who would enter our country to terrorize Americans. But the solution to the problem of illegal immigration is not simply to close our borders. The solution is to welcome legal immigrants and legal legitimate refugees, and to turn away those who do not obey the laws. We must say no to illegal immigration so we can continue to say yes to legal immigration.[6]

The President's remarks, and the policy changes he outlined that day, were tailored to very immediate public concerns about illegal immigrants. The special emphasis on immigrant smuggling ("traffic in human cargo") responded to public dismay at the June 1993 grounding off Long Island, New York, of the *Golden Venture*—a freighter packed with desperate Chinese migrants traveling under wretched conditions and bound, illegally, for America. (In the months that followed, several more boatloads of smuggled Chinese were discovered offshore.) The President proposed counterterrorist measures in answer to public outrage about the February 1993 bombing of New York's World Trade Center, in which legal and illegal immigrants from the Middle East were believed to be involved. And better enforcement at the borders (the President proposed increased funding for the Border Patrol) responded to feverish concerns about illegal Mexican migrants pouring across the border into Texas and California.

Mexican Migrants and IRCA. Worrying about illegal immigration in America isn't new. In recent years, most of this concern has focused on immigration from Mexico, which has played a unique role in American history. Beginning in 1942, a series of programs allowed Mexicans to migrate temporarily into the United States for agricultural work. These workers, called braceros, flowed back and forth across the border in great numbers to meet seasonal demands for farm labor. These programs didn't eliminate illegal migration across the border (more Mexicans applied than the programs permitted entry, and some U.S. employers preferred to hire cheaper illegal labor), but they did reduce it. The bracero programs ended in 1964—but the flow of labor continued, only now much more of it was illegal.

The Immigration Reform and Control Act (IRCA) of 1986 was designed to address this massive and growing problem of undocumented workers. It granted amnesty to illegal immigrants who could document that they had lived in the United States continuously since before 1982, and to certain agricultural workers under a different set of standards. About 1.8 million applied for am-

A border patrol guard leads a group
of illegal aliens from Mexico into custody.
Among Mexicans, such officers are known
as la migra, and the dusty hills they police
between countries, las lomas.

nesty under IRCA's regular program, and 1.3 million under the agricultural program. Most of the applicants were men, nearly three quarters were Mexican, and nearly half were married.[7]

IRCA also made it illegal, as of 1988, to hire an illegal immigrant. Employers were required to complete a form for each new hire, certifying that they had reviewed the employee's legal documents. Employers who persisted in hiring illegals were subject to fines, and even to criminal penalties for repeated offenses.

IRCA clearly put a dent in illegal immigration. But easily counterfeited documents and lax enforcement of the law have limited IRCA's effectiveness.

And IRCA didn't alter the penalty for entering the country illegally: The only penalty for the migrant is deportation, and nothing prevents a deportee from simply turning around and trying to enter the United States again—and again. IRCA notwithstanding, the number of illegal immigrants keeps rising.

Who Are They, and How Do They Get Here? Who are these three million or so people living in the United States illegally? Their characteristics change as U.S. immigration policy and world migration patterns change. By the late 1980s and early 1990s, this was a fair description:

The typical illegal alien is about as likely to be non-Mexican as Mexican; about as likely to be a woman as a man. Most are permanently settled in the United States and reside with immediate family members; most are not employed in agriculture; and most face the same labor market opportunities as demographically comparable legal immigrants.[8]

George J. Borjas
Friends or Strangers

Illegal immigrants fall into several broad categories. EWIs (Immigration and Naturalization Service jargon for "entry without inspection") are those who have entered the country without having their travel documents inspected at the border. EWIs typically come in by land from Mexico, as it's virtually impossible to enter the United States through an airport without presenting documents for inspection. "Visa abusers" enter legally on tourist or student visas, then remain after their visas expire. Visa abusers are typically from overseas.

In addition to visa abusers and EWIs, still more illegal immigrants enter the country each year by presenting counterfeit documents for inspection. Many of these migrants (100,000 per year, the INS estimates) purchase their documents from smugglers.[9]

How Much Does Illegal Immigration Cost? Illegal immigrants are eligible for few services beyond the basic amenities (mass transit, police and fire protection, and so forth) available to everyone living in America. They are not eligible for such federal benefit programs as Aid to Families With Dependent Children (AFDC) and unemployment insurance. Most, however, help pay for these programs through federal taxes that are withheld from their paychecks. Some state and local health and welfare programs are open to illegals, and others quietly or carelessly admit them by failing to systematically check applicants' immigration status.

Two important benefits are guaranteed to illegal immigrants and their families. Federal law has required, since 1985, that health care providers not turn away anyone—including illegal immigrants—who needs emergency treatment. And the Supreme Court, in *Pliler* v. *Doe,* 1982, has ruled that all children are entitled to a free public education regardless of their immigration status.

California governor Pete Wilson (left) and an immigration officer survey counterfeit passports and identification cards used by illegal immigrants. Wilson pressed President Bill Clinton to experiment with tamper-proof immigrant ID cards in California. Many of Wilson's views on immigration sparked controversy.

Although it's obviously hard to measure this, many researchers have concluded that—with the likely exception of school costs—illegal immigrants, like legal immigrants, pay more in taxes than they collect in government benefits.[10] But, also as with legal immigrants, most of the illegals' tax money goes to the federal government while many of the services they use are paid for locally.

California picks up more of this cost than any other state. According to the U.S. Census Bureau, in 1993 as many as 2 million illegal immigrants were living in California—a state with a total population of 31.5 million.[11] "In the city of Los Angeles," Governor Pete Wilson noted, ". . . we have a community of illegal immigrants who, with their children, number almost a million people."[12] Wilson estimated that illegal immigrants and their children (American as well as foreign-born) cost California's taxpayers $2.3 billion per year just in money spent on education, emergency health care, and costs of imprisonment.[13] In 1992, Wilson asked (in vain) that the federal government pay for federally mandated services for legal as well as illegal immigrants. (Two years later California as well as Florida, Arizona, and Texas sued the federal government to recover some of these costs.) In 1993 he proposed dramatically changing the way we treat illegal residents.

Governor Wilson urged that the U.S. Constitution be changed to deny American citizenship to American-born children of parents who are here illegally. (All children born in the United States are automatically American citizens. Some critics of this longstanding policy complain that it encourages illegal immigrants to give birth in this country so that at least their children will be eligible to live here.) Wilson also proposed that free public education be denied to the children of illegals—whether the children were born in the United States or not. He advocated deporting illegals who sought emergency medical treatment (and having the federal government pick up the tab for the medical costs), asked that the government create a "tamper-proof" system of immigrant identification cards, and urged stronger policing on both sides of the U.S.-Mexican border.[14]

To those who disagree with him, Wilson's proposals raise disturbing questions about what sort of a country America should be. Wilson's critics also point out that some of his proposals could have unintended consequences that would not be in our best national interests. Might effectively denying health care to illegal immigrants endanger public health by spreading disease, especially since large numbers of illegal workers' jobs involve handling food, working in other people's homes, and caring for children? Or might refusing citizenship and education to the children of immigrants discourage family immigration and increase the number of illegal workers migrating alone? Over time, this could prove harmful: Immigrants who come here with their families generally assimilate better and in the long run make a greater economic and social contribution to America.[15]

Finally, Wilson's critics say, his proposals might not even reduce illegal immigration. Migrants, illegal and legal alike, come here to pursue better job opportunities than they have at home. Even if we eliminated all individual government benefits to illegal immigrants, many would still find it worth their while to come here.

7

Asylum

Anyone arriving in the United States who asks for asylum from persecution (a threat of harm that violates basic human rights) has a legal right, under American as well as international law, to pursue that claim through an American immigration court. Granting asylum to those who need it is an ancient international custom, and in recent years the United States has generously honored it. But how many of today's asylum claims come from people seeking to take unfair advantage of this system, people who know that a fraudulent claim of asylum can provide an opportunity to live and work in the United States for months or even years while the claim is being processed?

Abuse of the Asylum Process. Foreigners inside U.S. borders can legally seek asylum at any time, regardless of their immigration status—even after deportation proceedings against them have begun. Some people (including the Egyptian Muslim cleric Sheik Omar Abdel-

Rahman, who with some of his followers was charged in the World Trade Center bombing) request asylum once all their other legal options for remaining in the United States run out. Others—EWIs or visa abusers— live here illegally until they get caught, and only then claim asylum.

Our immigration system offers strong incentives to file for asylum. Asylees (people who are seeking or have been granted asylum), like refugees, are eligible for many social services (health care, English classes, job placement assistance—even cash grants) not offered to other immigrants. And, for those who don't have close relatives who are U.S. citizens and who don't fit any of the preference categories for admission (or who can't or don't want to spend years on a waiting list), being accepted as a refugee or asylee is just about the only legal way to settle here. (Under U.S. law a refugee is someone who has applied for and been granted asylum before coming to America. Those who apply *after* they've entered the United States—or at the border— are called asylees.)

Much of the concern in the early 1990s about abuse of the asylum system was focused on those who claimed asylum upon landing at John F. Kennedy International Airport, in New York. The asylum process at JFK— and at other U.S. ports of entry—went like this: An immigrant at the airport would ask for asylum based on some claim of political persecution. Officials from the Immigration and Naturalization Service, a branch of the U.S. Justice Department, then would decide whether or not the asylum seeker was to be imprisoned before having his or her case heard by a judge. (New York-area immigrant detention facilities were so overfilled by 1992 and 1993 that very few new claimants were held.) Typi-

*Children in El Salvador look out
from a building ravaged by that country's
civil war during the 1980s. Among the
many Salvadorans who sought asylum in
the United States were teenage boys, who
faced being forced into either the government's army or that of its leftist opponent.*

cally, the asylum seeker was given INS papers permitting him or her to live and work in the United States while waiting for a hearing scheduled months, at least, after his or her arrival. By 1993, most asylum claimants coming in through JFK weren't showing up for their hearings.

Undoubtedly some, perhaps many, of these asylum seekers were taking advantage of an overloaded system. The INS in 1993 had only 150 asylum officers handling about 135,000 new cases that year (about 15,000 of them originating at JFK and other U.S. airports) while trying to catch up with a huge backlog from previous years.

International Law and Custom. We can't simply say, "No more," and send asylum seekers back whence they came. Not only would it be morally unacceptable to send victims of torture and people who have received death threats back to their tormentors, but it would violate our obligations under international law.

Every state that belongs to the United Nations is required to take whatever actions are necessary to uphold the principles outlined in the 1948 Universal Declaration of Human Rights. Article 14.1 of this declaration explicitly covers asylum: "Everyone has the right to seek and enjoy in other countries asylum from persecution."[1]

International law and custom concerning refugees and asylees has evolved in response to changing international conditions. In 1951, a United Nations agreement addressed the problem of post-World War II refugees in Europe, many of whom were citizens of countries that no longer existed by the end of the war. A 1967 United Nations agreement (ratified by the United States in 1968) expanded the earlier convention's scope to include refugees worldwide.

These agreements committed the nations that ratified them to observing the right of "non-refoulement"—the right not to be sent back involuntarily to a country one has fled. Non-refoulement includes the right to seek asylum with another nation if one nation refuses it; in no case is a refugee to be forced to go home.

In addition to explicit international laws, certain generally observed customs have developed concerning refugees and asylees. Although victims of persecution have a right to asylum, each state retains the right to decide who does and who does not deserve to claim that right—to decide who is a legitimate refugee or asylee. Asylum is granted, at each state's discretion, not only to those fleeing persecution but also to people displaced by natural disaster or by war.

A nation sometimes refuses to grant asylum to a group of migrants that other nations perceive as legitimate refugees, seeking to avoid the heavy burden (or, in some cases, the political embarrassment) of taking them in. Thailand, for example, refused to recognize as refugees most Cambodians fleeing civil war in 1979 and forced 40,000 of them back across the border.[2] More recently, the United States has been criticized for summarily refusing asylum to Haitians and, during the 1980s, to migrants from several war-torn Central American countries.

The best option for resolving a refugee crisis is for the refugees to return to their homeland—but that requires resolving the problem that prompted them to flee in the first place. This does sometimes happen; occasionally, it happens on a very large scale. In 1972, for example, ten million Bengalis who had fled to India from Pakistan during the preceding civil war returned home to the new nation of Bangladesh (formerly East Pakistan).[3]

Refugees often seek to settle in neighboring countries, where the culture, climate, geography, and language may be familiar to them. This can impose a huge burden on nations that may be suffering from the same pressures that created the refugee crisis nearby. And concentrating large numbers of refugees near their troubled homeland can foster or spread war, with fighters recruiting from the refugee camps or using them as safe havens for soldiers.

When a refugee crisis sets adrift too many people to be absorbed by neighboring states, other nations are called upon to share the burden. Nations all around the world, and especially the United States, accepted 1.5 million refugees who fled Cambodia, Laos, and Vietnam between 1975 and 1980.[4]

The international response to a refugee crisis addresses two tasks: The first action must be to provide enough immediate food, medical, and other humanitarian aid to make manageable the burden of the government that is sheltering the refugees. Then the international community must make it possible for the refugees to find permanent places to settle and ways to support themselves, either back in their homeland, in the country they've fled to, or in a third country. The United States has often played a generous role in these humanitarian efforts.

U.S. Law: The Refugee Act of 1980. Before 1980, most refugees who came to the United States were admitted under special acts of Congress or administrative actions in response to specific crises abroad. (Under the Displaced Persons Act of 1948, for example, hundreds of thousands of World War II refugees were admitted.) The Refugee Act of 1980, coming on the heels of a series of refugee crises in the 1970s, was designed to bring order to this haphazard system for processing refugees abroad and to reconcile U.S. law with international law. Echoing the language of the United Nations, the Refugee Act defined a refugee as someone living outside his or her country and unable or unwilling to return due to a "well-founded fear of persecution on account of race, religion, nationality, membership in a social group, or political opinion." (In contrast, the 1965 U.S. immigration legislation had defined a refugee as someone fleeing persecution from a Communist, Communist-dominated, or Middle Eastern government. Few people applied at the border for asylum under this law—an average of 200 per year between 1968 and 1975—but those who applied were routinely admitted.)[5] The 1980 legislation required the U.S. government to use a single standard in considering all applications for asylum, regardless of the applicant's nationality or politics, or whether the person was in the country legally or illegally. Only a limited number of refugees were to be admitted after being processed overseas, and individual refugees had to meet the health and other requirements applied to all immigrants under U.S. law.

The Refugee Act established two different procedures for determining refugee status—one for applicants overseas, and the other for applicants at the border or within the United States. Each year the president, in consultation with Congress, sets limits on how many refugees overseas are to be given permission to enter the United States that year from various regions (Africa, East Asia, eastern Europe, etc.). These ceilings can be—and usually are—revised later in the year to adjust to changing international conditions.

Refugees around the world apply to the U.S. government for the limited number of refugee visas available. Those who fit the definition of "refugee" set out

"Can you *prove* that you're
'tempest-tost'?"

*This cartoon satirizes the restrictions
placed on asylum seekers after the
Refugee Act of 1980.*

in the 1980 Refugee Act *and* who are not otherwise excludable (for being HIV-positive, for example) are admitted in numbers up to the regional ceiling. From Africa, for example, during the year ending in September 1993 no more than six thousand refugees were to be given permission to come to the United States—no matter how many qualified people applied.

Those refugees who are granted permission to come to the United States become eligible to apply for permanent resident status one year after they arrive, and most apply soon after they become eligible. During the year ending in September 1993, 123,010 refugees arrived in the United States. In that same year, 117,037 refugees became permanent legal residents; most of these had arrived a year or two earlier. Five years after their arrival, refugees who have become legal permanent residents may apply to become naturalized citizens.

Asylum seekers follow a different procedure. Like refugees, asylees must demonstrate "a well-founded fear of persecution," and they must not violate any of the law's grounds for exclusion. But unlike refugees, asylum seekers are already in the United States, and—most important—there's no legal limit on how many people can be granted asylum each year. The number of people who have applied for asylum has risen steeply in recent years. Here's how the INS describes the asylum procedure:

Any alien physically present in the United States or at a port of entry may request asylum in the United States. According to the [1980] Refugee Act, current immigration status, whether legal or illegal, is not relevant to an individual's asylum claim. An alien may apply for asylum in one of two ways: with an INS asylum officer, or, if apprehended [for being in the country illegally], with an immigration judge in a deportation or exclusion hearing.

Asylum procedures require that an INS officer interview each applicant and consult with the Bureau of Human Rights and Humanitarian Affairs (Department of State) for an advisory opinion on every asylum case. There are no limits set by law on the number of individuals who may be granted asylum in the United States [each year]. An alien denied asylum by the INS may appeal the denial to an immigration judge during deportation or exclusion proceedings.[6]

Statistical Yearbook
of the INS 1992

Asylum seekers are permitted to live in the United States while their applications are being processed—and this can take years. (In 1994, the INS announced tighter restrictions on work permits for asylum seekers, as well as streamlined procedures intended to greatly speed up processing.) If asylum is granted, one year later asylees may apply for permanent resident status; four years after that, they may apply to become citizens.

Politics and Asylum Seekers. During the 1980s, large numbers of people claiming political asylum began to come to the United States from nations to which few or none of the normal overseas refugee visas had been assigned. (From the mid-1970s to the mid-1980s, most refugee visas were reserved for Southeast Asians. Beginning in 1988, large numbers of refugees from the Soviet Union, many of them Russian Jews, were accommodated. Few visas were assigned to African and Latin American nations.) Many asylum seekers came from countries whose repressive governments maintained cordial relations with the U.S. government. Most of those applicants were, initially at least, denied asylum, and it came to be widely believed that people coming from certain nations (Guatemala, Haiti, and El Salvador especially) were routinely treated unfairly by the U.S. asylum system.

Refugees from Communist Cuba, for example, have been welcomed in the United States, while people fleeing repressive but non-Communist Haiti have been turned away. In 1993, the Supreme Court upheld the Clinton administration's decision to continue the policy, begun under President Ronald Reagan, of preventing Haitian asylum seekers intercepted at sea from reaching U.S. shores. However, in 1994 President Clinton modified the policy and agreed to give Haitians intercepted at sea hearings on ships or in other Caribbean nations. Cubans were no longer automatically admitted.

Asylum seekers from El Salvador and Guatemala in the 1980s found that an overburdened INS and a hostile State Department added up to overwhelming odds against asylum. Between 1983 and 1989, only 2 percent of Guatemalans and 2.5 percent of Salvadorans seeking asylum were granted it.[7] Some reported being pressured to leave the United States "voluntarily" without applying for asylum. Often those who did apply, like Mr. R., a Salvadoran, were told that their experiences did not fit the official definition of "persecution":

Mr. R. worked actively over several years for political and social reform in El Salvador. He helped to establish the Committee of Marginalized Communities there, which he described as a group formed to aid earthquake victims in San Salvador.

Salvadoran security forces raided the committee's offices in July 1989. In August, more than a dozen armed men searched the San Salvador home of Mr. R.'s

mother. They abducted his brother, telling his mother
that when Mr. R. made himself available to them, they
would release his brother.

Armed men in civilian clothes later came to Mr.
R.'s residence. He was away from home at the time, but
that visit was followed by anonymous threats against
him. He and his wife then left El Salvador to seek asy-
lum in the United States.

Mr. R. applied for asylum in Harlingen, Texas,
near the Mexican border, in October 1989. The advi-
sory opinion of the [State Department's] Bureau of Hu-
man Rights and Humanitarian Affairs, issued within a
day of his application, stated that Mr. R. faced 'prose-
cution' rather than persecution in El Salvador. There-
fore, he was not eligible for asylum. He received notice
a few days later that the director of the INS district of-
fice intended to deny his asylum claim. The INS report-
edly granted him asylum only after concerned members
of the Texas community began a campaign of petitions
and protests on his behalf.[8]

Amnesty International USA
Reasonable Fear

Several human rights organizations have persistently focused public attention on the desperate circumstances of
asylum seekers and have pushed effectively for a more
generous interpretation of the asylum laws. Chief
among these organizations is Amnesty International, in-
fluential and well known for its reliable reports on human rights abuses and its huge membership (1.1 million
members at the end of 1993, about 400,000 in the
United States).[9]

In 1990, in an out-of-court settlement of a lawsuit,
the Justice Department agreed that Salvadorans and

Guatemalans who had not been granted asylum in the 1980s could reapply or have their cases reopened. The asylum system is now treating Central American asylum seekers more generously and fairly—but refugee advocates believe that many others, from nations as diverse as Haiti and Sri Lanka, are still being unfairly excluded.

Growing Numbers. In 1970, the number of refugees around the world was 2.5 million. By 1980, the total had climbed to 8 million, and (according to the UN High Commissioner for Refugees) by October 1993 a staggering 19.7 million refugees lived outside their homelands, with an additional 24 million displaced within their own countries. Most of these nearly 44 million migrants are women and their children.[10]

Before this great explosion in the world's refugee population, most refugees found asylum near their homelands, and few ever came to the United States. But with so many now seeking refuge, aided by cheap air travel, more and more are coming to America.

And not only to America. The collapse of the Soviet bloc has unleashed a flood of East European and central Asian refugees, mostly in the direction of western Europe. During 1991, 600,000 sought asylum in western Europe and North America. In 1992, Germany alone logged more than 500,000 asylum applications.[11]

Between 1980 and 1993, the American government spent $10.3 billion in resettling the 1.3 million refugees (up from only about half a million in the 1970s) admitted from around the world under the quota system. During this same period, only 56,000 asylum seekers who applied after arriving in the United States were granted asylum.[12] By 1993 the asylum system for applicants already in the United States was so overwhelmed that its backlog of unresolved cases numbered 300,000. (Nearly half of these cases derived from the lawsuit settlement with Guatemalans and Salvadorans.)[13]

How to Fix the System. The system for handling refugee claims made to U.S. officials overseas has for the most part worked smoothly. The issue of how to assign the limited number of visas, however, will probably be a source of future controversy. As more and more refugees scramble for safe havens, Americans seem less and less willing to accept greater numbers of immigrants. Disputes about how many refugees we should accept, and about how the limited number of refugee visas should be distributed, seem inevitable.

The system for handling refugee claims presented inside the United States clearly has *not* worked smoothly. Many proposals to deal with this have been raised among policy makers and debated publicly. The streamlined procedures announced in 1994 were intended to catch up with the INS backlog of asylum cases and to speed up the asylum appeal process. More changes in policy were expected. Whether the policy changes will adequately protect the right of asylum seekers to a fair hearing remains to be seen.

Fixing the process for handling claims, although obviously necessary, won't solve all our asylum problems. There remains the difficult matter of defining who should be considered a refugee. During the Cold War the answer seemed clear: People fleeing Communist oppression and victims of regional wars, which were often fought between Communists and anti-Communists, were eligible; economic migrants were not. Now the distinctions aren't so clear. Americans do not agree on what conditions match the legal definition of a "well-founded fear of persecution for reasons of race, religion, nationality, membership in a particular social group or political opinion"—and many worry that this definition of persecution might include far more people than they're willing to take in. Do anti-homosexual death squads in Brazil count? Does the Chinese policy of limiting families to one child per couple? (President George Bush decreed that it did, and in January 1994 a federal court upheld that policy as it applied to several asylum seekers.[14]) What about the custom of female genital mutilation practiced in parts of Africa?

More confusing still, the situations that now produce mass migrations of refugees typically *combine* great economic hardship, political oppression, violence, environmental devastation, and sometimes natural disasters. as well. In many cases it is hard to say whether political or economic or other factors offer the stronger push. Ultimately, solving the problems of the way we handle asylum—and the way we handle all immigration—will require us to revise not only U.S. immigration policy and law but our foreign policy and our view of the world as well.

8
Shaping the Stream of Newcomers

Generally we believe that it's a good thing, both economically and as a personal freedom, when people are *able* to migrate, but a terrible misfortune when people *need* to migrate because it's impossible for them to live where they are. The United States' wealth and relatively strong economy make it an attractive destination for voluntary migrants and refugees alike. How many and which migrants choose to try to come here are determined to a great extent not only by our domestic immigration policy but by U.S. foreign policy as well.

Our immigration policy boils down to three questions: How many people should we admit? Who should they be? And how should we implement our policy; that is, what measures should we take to give visas to those who should have them and to keep others out? How we answer these questions will depend on the importance we assign to various economic, political, and humanitarian goals.

How Many Should We Admit? One third of the annual population growth of the United States now comes from immigration, and 20 to 25 percent of that immigration is illegal.[1] If we include immigrants' American-born children, immigrants and their children make up more than half of our population growth.[2] In recent years, immigrants on average—although not all nationalities of immigrants—have had a higher birthrate than native-born Americans.

The birthrate among native-born American women has decreased to a bare replacement rate of 2.0 children per woman. Assuming that Americans continue to have children at this rate, without immigration the population of the United States would stop growing by the middle of the twenty-first century.[3]

America is a relatively uncrowded place, compared with many parts of the world. How many people can our country comfortably support? Increasing our population through immigration means increasing our need for new infrastructure and services (such as roads and schools). But it also offers us the chance to benefit from more of the energy and labor and new ideas that immigration has brought us throughout our history. Furthermore, in the future, as our population ages, we might well need a continuing infusion of young immigrant workers to help support our growing number of retirees.

Whom Should We Admit? Economic policy, and characteristics of our economy that have nothing to do with our official immigration policy, have a huge impact on which and how many immigrants come here. For example, our less-progressive income tax (with relatively low taxes on the wealthy compared to taxes in other developed countries) might help pull in high-income immigrants. Similarly, our relatively high minimum wage, compared with wages in developing nations, probably attracts low-income workers from those countries. Whether we intend it or not, the mix of immigrants America attracts will inevitably be influenced by any changes here or abroad that affect the differences between the wages and economic opportunities of American workers—skilled or unskilled—and their counterparts elsewhere.

But not only does the state of our economy shape immigration patterns; immigration policy affects the economy as well. Our current policy's strong bias in favor of family unification probably has a mixed effect on our economy. On one hand, some highly talented and productive individuals probably have been blocked from coming to the United States because they have no family ties here. On the other hand, in recent years people who have come here as part of a migrating family unit have been on average more skilled (and thus better able to make a strong economic contribution) than lone migrants.

A different policy—say, one biased toward workers with certain skills—would have a different economic impact. Although the proportions of skilled and unskilled immigrants don't seem to much affect American wage and unemployment rates, they probably affect how much wealth and what kinds of products we create and certainly affect us as consumers. Are we better off having the cheaper food made possible by low-skill, low-wage immigrant farm workers, or would we be better off with cheaper, more advanced technology fashioned by more highly trained immigrants?

Unskilled workers have lower incomes, which means they contribute less to our national wealth and pay less in taxes. They are disproportionately poor and apt to go on welfare, so a flow of less-skilled immigrants lowering the average skill level of workers in the United States probably worsens all of our poverty-related problems. Although immigrants as a group do pay more in taxes than they cost in government services, might we want to change immigration policy to attract migrants who'll be able to pay even more?

Immigrants' advocates worry that more and more Americans only like immigrants after they've been in America long enough to move up the economic ladder—not when they first arrive. These advocates fear that restricting immigration may kill the dream of poor immigrants coming to America to make their fortunes, doing good for everyone by doing well for themselves.

Taking in immigrants does cost us money, at least in the short term. It has become a huge financial burden for regions such as California where large numbers of immigrants concentrate. Since the ultimate benefits of immigration are reaped by the nation as a whole, should we redistribute some of this initial burden? How much of it? Might spreading the burden reduce the growing hostility to immigrants in areas where they now concentrate? Or might spreading the burden just spread the hostility as well, as citizens of places such as Idaho and Vermont find themselves picking up part of the tab for local services in California, Florida, and New York?

Too Much Diversity? Between the 1920s and the 1960s the United States used immigration policy to maintain a fairly stable mix of ethnic groups in the U.S. population. Since then, we've become vastly more diverse. Some people worry that we've become too diverse, that some immigrants (specifically, non-Europeans) may be too "foreign" to be assimilated into the United States in large numbers. Is this a problem? Clearly immigrants rooted in cultures very different from ours have bigger adjustments to make. For example, an immigrant from England or Canada—English-speaking, accustomed to the demands of a developed capitalist economy, familiar with many holidays celebrated in the United States—will obviously find adjusting easier than, say, a refugee from Somalia or China. Is it xenophobic (unreasonably fearful of outsiders), racist, and even un-American to worry about this? Or is it anti-American *not* to worry about it?

Most Americans have become vastly more tolerant of diversity, or at least much less willing to appear intolerant. Diversity has become fashionable. The old ideal of the melting pot (different ethnic groups blending together and becoming indistinguishable) has been elbowed aside by the image of an American mosaic: different ethnic groups living side by side while retaining their distinctive ethnic characteristics.

Yet we worry about some groups of immigrants remaining forever apart, alien elements not integrated into our society. Does our ideal of tolerance of diversity, by relieving some of the pressure to conform, discourage assimilation? Might this in the long run make it harder for America to absorb more newcomers?

By one important measure—citizenship—recent immigrants are less assimilated than their predecessors. Fifty years ago, most immigrants routinely applied to become naturalized U.S. citizens after they became eligible. By the early 1990s, only about one third of those eligible were applying to become citizens;[4] the INS estimated that ten million legal permanent residents had not become U.S. citizens. (In November 1993, the INS announced that, for the first time, the U.S. government would actively encourage immigrants to become citizens, in part to help cool growing American hostility toward immigrants—especially Mexican immigrants—

relatively few of whom had been applying for citizenship.[5])

Different naturalization rates, between recent and less-recent immigrants as well as among different ethnic groups, may be largely due to different degrees of difficulty—practical as well as political—in returning home, or even maintaining contact with the homeland. Recently arrived Asians, for example, are much more likely to become citizens than immigrants from Canada or Mexico. And decades ago, when naturalization was more common, travel was much more expensive and telephones much less widely available and affordable than they are today.

The apparent non-assimilation of immigrants living in Spanish-speaking enclaves has excited special concern. Newly arrived immigrants have often concentrated in ethnic enclaves in this country, and native-born Americans throughout our history have worried that these immigrants might never become fully part of America. But ethnic enclaves have played an important role in helping newcomers to assimilate, by providing job opportunities, role models, informal advice about living in America, and access to appropriate service organizations. Ultimately, of course, most immigrants who have lived in enclaves have moved into the American mainstream—or their children have done so. Nonetheless, does the sheer number of Spanish speakers, and the size of many Hispanic enclaves, make their case qualitatively different? If so, what should we do about the situation?

The children of recent immigrants have demonstrated that assimilation hasn't stopped. They do learn their parents' native languages and are generally bilingual—but most speak English best. (Earlier immigrants, under greater pressure to blend in, less frequently taught ancestral languages to their children.) Even most children living in immigrant enclaves (where it's possible to get by without knowing English) speak English, thanks largely to public schooling.[6]

Attracting the Immigrants We Want. Any immigration policy (except a completely open door) is inherently discriminatory. Making policy is about choosing on what basis we want to discriminate. Our current system discriminates heavily in favor of relatives of United States citizens and legal residents. Other countries do it differently.

Canada and Australia, for example, use a point system by which applicants for immigration are graded according to education, age, occupation, and other factors. Only high scorers are admitted. We might consider such a system, awarding points for such characteristics as those and others, perhaps including English fluency and special skills. We could, over time, tinker with what gets awarded points, to meet changing needs.

There are problems with this approach. A point system is imprecise: Immigrants with the same formal qualifications are not necessarily equally skilled, and depending on how the qualifications are defined we might not end up favoring the applicants intended. Further, a point system doesn't address the question of how to attract the applicants we want—it only lets us choose among those who have chosen to apply. And deciding how to assign points could be politically explosive and socially divisive. Would points for English fluency be seen as a racist tactic designed to exclude Latinos? Might other point assignments be seen as anti-Asian or anti-African?

A point system might work best for America if it included some elements of our existing immigration policy. It might, for example, give extra points to family members or to groups of migrants we especially wish to favor for humanitarian reasons. Or we might allocate only a fraction of all immigrant visas to a point system, with other blocks of visas to be allocated to family members and refugees.

A completely different approach would be to *sell* visas, at a fixed price or even to the highest bidder. People who could afford to buy visas would more likely be wealthy and well educated, and certainly such an approach would bring in money that could be used to offset immediate immigrant settlement costs.

But there are problems with selling visas. It might encourage immigrants to come here with huge debts that would reduce their ability to invest in America. And would it be fair? Most of our ancestors couldn't have come here if they'd had to pay large sums to enter. Such a policy might also work against our long-term best interests, by screening out ambitious start-up entrepreneurs and failing to give enough credit for the nonmonetary contributions immigrants make to America. Worse, it probably wouldn't work. The 1990 immigration legislation set aside 10,000 visas per year for "yacht people"—immigrants willing to invest substantial sums in American business. Few have applied, and very few have arrived—only 59 in the year ending in September 1993.[7]

Keeping Out Those We Don't Want. To reduce the number of asylees living in the United States, perhaps we'll move toward a system of granting temporary sanctuary to many applicants, with no permanent right to U.S. residence, combined with efforts to create acceptable conditions under which refugees could return home. United States law already permits the federal government to grant a form of temporary sanctuary. Expanding the use of this option might make the admirable humanitarian goal of giving refuge to more of the world's neediest people more agreeable to the American public. But it begs the question of how many of today's refugees can realistically be expected to return home safely any time soon.

As for stopping illegal immigration at the border, many measures have been discussed recently. To pay for any new measures, Congress can either take money out of existing tax revenues or find new sources of money, such as by increasing the fee (raised to $6.50 in 1994) paid by travelers entering the United States.[8]

Other proposals for keeping illegal immigrants out, such as lengthier interrogations at the Mexican border, are controversial. More controversial still are any of various stronger measures suggested to find and deport illegals who are already in the country. Would we be willing to carry cards verifying our citizenship or legal immigrant status at all times or risk detention? Would we allow INS agents to stop "foreign-looking" pedestrians, or people on the street at random, to demand identification?

Operation Blockade. Operation Blockade, set up along the Mexican border at El Paso, Texas, is an example of a tough (and effective) approach to controlling our borders. It also illustrates that extreme immigration policies can have powerful and unintended consequences.

Two sister cities, El Paso, Texas, and Ciudad Juarez, Mexico, face each other across the Rio Grande. Before Operation Blockade, Border Patrol agents arrested and deported Mexicans who crossed the river without the proper papers—if they could catch them. Beginning in September 1993, however, the Border Patrol took a different approach: They began to *prevent* anyone from even trying to cross the border illegally. Four hundred agents deployed along 20 miles (32 kilometers) of the border arrested more than eight hundred illegal entrants a day, at first; by Thanksgiving, when word had spread that the entire stretch of border near El Paso was covered, arrests were down to around forty a day.

Clearly the program worked. Far fewer Mexicans entered El Paso without having their papers inspected. Many El Paso residents believed that this kept out at least some unquestionably unwelcome visitors: Car theft, pickpocketing, shoplifting, and burglary all decreased in downtown El Paso after the blockade took effect.

But far more Mexicans were now trying to enter El Paso, legally or illegally, via the only way left open to them: through the INS inspection stations at the bridges between the two cities. Even though the Border Patrol added extra agents to check papers at the bridges (many phony documents were confiscated), crossing a bridge—which used to be a five-minute formality—became an hours-long ordeal.

Thousands of Mexicans used to cross the border legally every day, to work or to shop in El Paso. Many continued to do so, enduring the long lines and added hassle at the border. But many decided that it wasn't worth the effort. Large retailers saw their sales drop 10 to 15 percent, while merchants who catered to Mexican shoppers saw their sales cut by half or more.

Operation Blockade seems also to have turned many illegal *commuters* into illegal *immigrants*. Undocumented workers who did make it across the border were reluctant to go home at night, for fear of being unable to cross the border to return to work the next day. Some agricultural workers slept in or near the fields. Other undocumented workers found more permanent shelter and tried, illegally, to bring their families in.

The far-reaching effects of Operation Blockade couldn't be measured entirely in numbers—number of arrests, number of sales made or lost, number of illegal immigrants. The citizens of El Paso and Juarez used to speak of themselves as brothers and sisters, their cities as two parts of one interdependent community. Operation Blockade redefined life in this community. Many people worried that it would permanently sour cross-border business and social relationships. Many wondered whether, in the long run, they would look back and think it was a mistake.

Fortress Europe. Migration is an international problem, and dealing with it will require international cooperation. The United States can't effectively go it alone. The United Nations has played, and will continue to play, an important role in coordinating the world's response to migration crises. But much of this response comes down to the domestic and foreign policies of individual nations. American policies will more likely be effective if they work in concert with those of other nations, especially the world's developed nations, and most especially western Europe, where public attitudes and government policies have been changing radically in response to the world migration crisis.

After World War II, the countries of northwestern Europe actively encouraged the immigration of cheap labor from southern Europe, northern Africa, and Turkey. These migrants were viewed as temporary "guest" workers, even though many stayed for decades. Their welcome began to run out during the 1970s oil crisis (when producers of much of the world's oil cooperated to raise prices dramatically), which was a terrific eco-

*Nazi skinheads protesting in Germany.
In the early 1990s, immigrants in Germany
were harassed and even killed by members
of these neo-Nazi groups.*

nomic shock to Europe. European countries tightened their immigration restrictions. Hostility to foreign workers has since grown, as Europe's economies have weakened and unemployment has risen through the 1980s and into the 1990s.

Nonetheless, workers from the Mediterranean countries still seek work in western Europe. And in the 1990s they've been joined by a flood of migrants from the formerly Communist states to the east. Many in western Europe are now calling for "zero immigration." Hostility—even violence—against immigrants and anyone else who looks "foreign" has risen in such liberal democracies as Germany, France, and Britain, and official policy toward migrants has become much more restrictive.

Since the collapse of communism, 200,000 Albanians have fled to Greece; thousands of them have been rounded up and bused back across the border. In France, where (as in the United States) children born on French soil have traditionally been considered citizens, the French-born children of immigrants must now formally apply for citizenship between the ages of sixteen and twenty one.[9]

The most striking of the recent changes have come in Germany, which absorbed nearly half a million immigrants in 1992, thanks largely to its asylum policy, then the most generous in Europe. In July 1993, Germany's asylum policy became one of the tightest in Europe: All who arrive by air are turned back if their homelands are classified by the German government as free of political persecution, and no one who on his or her route to Germany passes through a "safe third country" (a category that includes all of the countries that border Germany) is to be admitted. Since this policy change took effect, the number of those seeking asylum in Germany has plummeted—but at the same time the number of illegal aliens has risen.[10]

In an effort to hold back the rising tide of immigration, the twelve western, developed countries of the European Community have agreed to create a "Fortress Europe" by coordinating their immigration policies to keep foreigners out. At the end of 1993, restrictions at the internal borders among these twelve countries were to be loosened, while control of the external borders (those borders between these twelve nations and *other* nations) was to be greatly strengthened.[11]

This may reduce immigration to Europe, or it may simply increase the proportion of migrants who settle there illegally. In any event, Fortress Europe won't reduce the growing number of those who *want* to migrate; it may, by limiting their options in Europe, increase the number who come to America.

U.S. Foreign Policy. The single greatest step the United States could take toward resolving its immigration problems, and possibly the greatest humanitarian achievement the nation could accomplish, would be to reduce the total number of migrants around the world by reducing their needs to migrate. Policies that promote international stability, discourage violence and encourage peaceful resolution of disputes, work toward stabilizing population growth, encourage the recognition of human rights, promote economic growth and equitable economic opportunity, and protect the environment all would serve this crucial long-term goal.

It's tempting to believe that economic migration can be headed off simply by bringing industry to less-developed countries, taking advantage of their cheap labor. Often, however, this kind of development has produced little long-term benefit for the developing country. And much development has *increased* migration, from rural areas to the factories, and then—as the factory towns' populations have outgrown their economic opportunities—from less-developed to more-developed regions. A foreign policy targeted toward boosting *rural* economic development might be more successful in promoting equitable opportunity and reducing the need for migration.

American involvement in other nations' civil conflicts, especially during the Cold War, has also helped to generate large flows of migrants. Our asylum system is still clogged with cases of this kind that originated in Central America in the 1980s, when U.S. military aid fueled several civil wars. Obviously, a foreign policy that promotes peace (and encourages other nations to do so as well), instead of giving combatants the means to prolong fighting, is likely to reduce the number of migrants fleeing civil conflict.

In recent years, long-suppressed ethnic, religious, and other cultural conflicts have blown up into full-scale civil wars in areas previously dominated by communism (Yugoslavia and parts of the former Soviet Union) or by Cold War rivalries (Angola and other Third World nations). Combatants in many of these conflicts have tapped into the military infrastructure left behind after the Cold War. These ethnic clashes have loosed large numbers of migrants, especially from areas such as the former Yugoslavia where one ethnic group has fought to "cleanse" (remove) people of other ethnic groups from certain territory.

Resolving ethnic conflicts after they've escalated into war has proved difficult indeed. Perhaps U.S. foreign policy can more successfully help to *prevent* future armed clashes, by seeking ways to cool off ancient hatreds and encourage respect for human rights. Ways to

An Afghan grocer in New York City reflects the growing diversity newcomers have brought to the United States.

do this might include enforcing respect for existing international boundaries (since there's no orderly international mechanism for redrawing them); encouraging governments to allow ethnic subgroups reasonable autonomy and to find agreeable ways to balance the needs of various groups within their countries; and strengthening governmental and nongovernmental multi-ethnic institutions built around common interests rather than ethnic identity.

Immigration touches all aspects of life in America. Immigration policy affects us all, often in ways that aren't immediately obvious. Paying attention to changes that affect immigration is an important part of looking after each of our best interests. The shape of our future is at stake.

Notes

Chapter One

1. Quoted in Public Agenda Foundation, *Immigration: What We Promised, Where to Draw the Line* (Dayton, Ohio: Domestic Policy Association, 1986), p. 21.
2. Thomas Paine, *Common Sense*, 1776.
3. George J. Borjas, *Friends or Strangers: The Impact of Immigrants on the U.S. Economy* (New York: Basic Books, 1990), p. 27.
4. Emma Lazarus, "The New Colossus," sonnet inscribed in 1903 on the base of the Statue of Liberty.
5. Borjas, p. 4.
6. Quoted in *Immigration: What We Promised*, pp. 18–19.
7. Quoted in Robert W. Fox and Ira H. Mehlman, *Crowding Out the Future: World Population Growth, U.S. Immigration, and Pressures on Natural Resources* (Washington, D.C.: Federation for American Immigration Reform, 1992), p. 24.
8. Speech delivered at the White House on June 18, 1993, quoted in *National Journal*, August 7, 1993, p. 1977.

Chapter Two

1. Office of United Nations High Commissioner for Refugees (UNHCR), press release, November 9, 1993.
2. United Nations Population Fund, *The State of the World Population 1993* (New York: UNFPA, 1993), p. 7.
3. *The State of the World Population 1993,* pp. 20, 25.
4. Jodi L. Jacobson, *Environmental Refugees: A Yardstick of Habitability,* Worldwatch Paper 86 (Washington, D.C.: Worldwatch Institute, 1988), pp. 15–16.
5. *The State of the World Population 1993,* p. 8.
6. *The Washington Post,* September 11, 1993.
7. UN figures cited in *Fox and Mehlman,* p. 2.
8. *The State of the World Population 1993,* pp. 9, 24.
9. A 1992 UN report cited in *The State of the World Population 1993,* p. 11.
10. *The State of the World Population 1993,* p. 13.
11. UN figures cited in *Fox and Mehlman,* p. 2.
12. Clive Ponting, *A Green History of the World: The Environment and the Collapse of Great Civilizations* (New York: Penguin Books, 1993), pp. 70–72.
13. Jacobson, p. 26.
14. Jacobson, p. 29.
15. *The State of the World Population 1993,* p. 17.
16. "Taking Refuge in Each Other: Resettled Somalis, Ethiopians Struggle to Cope with D.C.," *The Washington Post,* November 28, 1993, p. A1.
17. *The State of the World Population 1993,* p. 32.
18. *The State of the World Population 1993,* p. 18.
19. *Wall Street Journal* reporter James McGregor, "China in Transition: Mao to Markets," *MacNeil/Lehrer NewsHour,* Public Broadcasting System (PBS), November 9, 1993.
20. *The State of the World Population 1993,* p. 16.

Chapter Three

1. U.S. Bureau of the Census, *Historical Statistics of the United States: Colonial Times to 1957* (Washington, D.C.: Government Printing Office, 1960), p. 48.
2. Quoted in *Immigration: What We Promised,* p. 6.
3. Anne Loftis, *California—Where the Twain Did Meet* (New

York: Macmillan, 1973), pp. 164–165. Reprinted by permission of Macmillan Publishing Co.; copyright © 1973 by Anne Loftis.

4. *Historical Statistics*, p. 66.
5. *Historical Statistics*, p. 66.
6. *Historical Statistics*, p. 66.
7. *Historical Statistics*, p. 66.
8. *Immigration: What We Promised*, p. 19.
9. *Immigration: What We Promised*, pp. 6, 13.
10. Literature provided by museum at Ellis Island, undated.
11. Bronislawa Tanajewski Lenski, interview by Richard Andryszewski, audiotape, November 1993.

Chapter Four

1. INS figures cited in Borjas, p. 37.
2. Quoted in Borjas, p. 31.
3. *The State of the World Population 1993*, p. 17.
4. *Immigration: What We Promised*, p. 7.
5. Congressional Quarterly, 1990 *Almanac* (Washington, D.C.: CQ Books, 1991), pp. 482–484.
6. Borjas, pp. 192–196.
7. Borjas, p. 179.
8. U.S. Immigration and Naturalization Service, *Statistical Yearbook of the Immigration and Naturalization Service, 1992* (Washington, D.C.: Government Printing Office, 1993).
9. *The New York Times*, June 27, 1993.
10. *The Washington Post*, October 11, 1993, p. A1.
11. *The Washington Post*, July 5, 1993, p. A1.
12. *National Journal*, August 7, 1993, p. 1978; Center for National Policy, press release, August 12, 1993.
13. *National Journal*, August 7, 1993, p. 1978.

Chapter Five

1. CNN/*USA Today* poll reported in *National Journal*, July 24, 1993, p. 1900.
2. Borjas, p. 99.
3. Borjas, pp. 88–89.
4. Borjas, pp. 88–89.

5. Department of Labor, Bureau of Labor Statistics, telephone conversation with author, November, 1993.
6. *Friends or Strangers,* pp. 79–96.
7. Department of Labor, Bureau of Labor Statistics, by phone, November, 1993.
8. Borjas, p. 135.
9. Borjas, pp. 111, 136.
10. Borjas, pp. 139, 108–110.
11. Borjas, pp. 140, 52.
12. Borjas; *The New York Times,* August 25, 1993, and related stories; Urban Institute, "Effects of Immigration on Black Workers," *Policy and Research Report,* Summer 1993, pp. 8–9.
13. Borjas.
14. *The Washington Post,* July 10, 1993.
15. Borjas, pp. 154–155, 157–158.
16. A 1986 National Bureau of Economic Research paper, cited in Borjas, p. 42.
17. Borjas, p. 43.
18. *The Washington Post,* September 12, 1993.

Chapter Six

1. *The New York Times,* June 27, 1993.
2. *The Washington Post,* September 1, 1993.
3. *The New York Times,* September 3, 1993.
4. Letter to the editor from the National Immigration Forum, *The New York Times,* September 1, 1993.
5. *National Journal,* August 7, 1993, p. 1978.
6. President Bill Clinton, remarks at the White House concerning new measures proposed to deal with illegal immigration, July 27, 1993, White House transcript.
7. INS data cited in Borjas, p. 74.
8. Borjas, p. 56.
9. *The Washington Post,* July 5, 1993.
10. *Immigration: What We Promised,* p. 15.
11. *The Washington Post,* August 17, 1993.
12. "Evans and Novak," August 21, 1993.
13. *The Washington Post,* August 17, 1993; information supplied by Governor Pete Wilson's office, November 1993.

14. *The New York Times*, August 16, 1993; information supplied by Governor Wilson's office, November 1993.
15. *The Washington Post*, August 17, 1993.

Chapter Seven

1. Quoted in Amnesty International USA, *Reasonable Fear: Human Rights and United States Refugee Policy* (New York: AIUSA, 1990), p. 2.
2. Kathleen Newland, *Refugees: The New International Politics of Displacement*, Worldwatch Paper 43 (Washington, D.C.: Worldwatch Institute, 1981), p. 8.
3. Newland, pp. 14–15.
4. Newland, p. 18.
5. *The New York Times Magazine*, September 19, 1993.
6. *Statistical Yearbook of the INS 1992*, p. 76.
7. *Reasonable Fear*, p. 17.
8. *Reasonable Fear*, p. 15.
9. Figures from Amnesty International, January 1994.
10. Information supplied by UNHCR, November 1993.
11. OECD paper cited in *The State of the World Population 1993*, p. 20.
12. INS figures cited in *National Journal*, August 7, 1993, p. 1978.
13. *The New York Times Magazine*, September 19, 1993.
14. *The New York Times*, January 21, 1994.

Chapter Eight

1. *National Journal*, July 24, 1993, p. 1900.
2. Fox and Mehlman, p. 3.
3. Fox and Mehlman, p. 24.
4. *The New York Times*, July 25, 1993.
5. *The New York Times*, November 26, 1993.
6. *The New York Times*, June 29, 1993.
7. *Statistical Yearbook of the INS 1992*, p. 18.
8. *The Washington Post*, January 23, 1994.
9. *The New York Times*, August 10, 1993.
10. *The New York Times*, August 10 and September 8, 1993.
11. *The New York Times*, August 10, 1993.

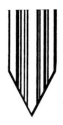

For Further
Information

Recommended Reading

Amnesty International USA. *Reasonable Fear: Human Rights and United States Refugee Policy.* New York: Amnesty International USA., 1990.

Benton, Barbara. *Ellis Island: A Pictorial History.* New York: Facts on File, 1985.

Bode, Janet. *New Kids on the Block: Oral Histories of Immigrant Teens.* New York: Franklin Watts, 1989.

Borjas, George J. *Friends or Strangers: The Impact of Immigrants on the U.S. Economy.* New York: Basic Books, 1990.

Dudley, William, ed. *Immigration: Opposing Viewpoints.* San Diego: Greenhaven, 1990.

Hauser, Pierre. *Illegal Aliens.* New York: Chelsea House, 1990.

Information Plus. *Immigration and Illegal Aliens: Burden or Blessing?* Wylie, Texas: Information Plus, 1991.

Jacobson, Jodi L. *Environmental Refugees: A Yardstick of Habitability*. Worldwatch Paper 86. Washington, D.C.: Worldwatch Institute, 1988.

Newland, Kathleen. *Refugees: The New International Politics of Displacement*. Worldwatch Paper 43. Washington, D.C.: Worldwatch Institute, 1981.

Public Agenda Foundation. *Immigration: What We Promised, Where to Draw the Line*. Dayton, Ohio: Domestic Policy Association, 1986.

United Nations Population Fund. *The State of the World Population 1993*. New York: UNFPA, 1993.

Organizations to Contact

Amnesty International USA, 322 Eighth Ave., New York, NY 10001.

Ellis Island Foundation, 52 Vanderbilt Ave., New York, NY 10017.

Federation for American Immigration Reform (FAIR), 1666 Connecticut Ave. NW, Washington, DC 20009.

Immigration and Naturalization Service, U.S. Department of Justice, 425 Eye St. NW, Washington, DC 20536.

National Immigration Forum, 220 Eye St. NE, Suite 220, Washington, DC 20002.

Public Agenda Foundation, National Issues Forum, 6 East 39th St., New York, NY 10016.

Index